Terry Waite has had a varied career and is best known as a hostage negotiator. He was also taken hostage himself in Beirut where he was kept in strict solitary confinement for almost five years. He has written about this experience in *Taken on Trust* (Hodder, 1993). He is also the author of *Footfalls in Memory* (Hodder, 1995) and two humorous books, *Travels with a Primate* (Hodder, 2000; Silvertail Books, 2014) and a comic novel, *The Voyage of the Golden Handshake* (Silvertail Books, 2015). He is a co-founder of Hostage UK and Y Care International and is president of Emmaus UK.

D1445822

# OUT OF THE SILENCE

## Memories, poems, reflections

Terry Waite

*Illustrations by Jenny Coles*

First published in Great Britain in 2016

Society for Promoting Christian Knowledge
36 Causton Street
London SW1P 4ST
www.spck.org.uk

Copyright © Terry Waite 2016
Illustrations copyright © Jenny Coles 2016

All rights reserved. No part of this book may be reproduced or transmitted in any
form or by any means, electronic or mechanical, including photocopying,
recording, or by any information storage and retrieval system,
without permission in writing from the publisher.

SPCK does not necessarily endorse the individual views contained in its publications.

Extracts taken or adapted from the Authorized Version of the Bible (The King James
Bible), the rights in which are vested in the Crown, are reproduced by permission
of the Crown's Patentee, Cambridge University Press.

The extract adapted from The Book of Common Prayer, the rights in which are
vested in the Crown, is reproduced by permission of the Crown's Patentee,
Cambridge University Press.

*British Library Cataloguing-in-Publication Data*
A catalogue record for this book is available from the British Library

ISBN 978–0–281–07761–8
eBook ISBN 978–0–281–07762–5

1 3 5 7 9 10 8 6 4 2

Typeset by Graphicraft Limited, Hong Kong

# Contents

| | | |
|---|---|---|
| *Preface* | | vii |
| *Introduction* | | ix |
| 1 | Another country | 1 |
| 2 | Evening | 5 |
| 3 | Dawn | 12 |
| 4 | Justice | 16 |
| 5 | Moods | 26 |
| 6 | Conflict | 29 |
| 7 | Ageing | 40 |
| 8 | Earthquake | 44 |
| 9 | Creators | 53 |
| 10 | Home | 56 |
| 11 | Family | 63 |
| 12 | Y Care | 73 |
| 13 | One to One | 76 |
| 14 | Belief | 80 |
| 15 | Anger | 87 |
| 16 | Relationships | 91 |
| 17 | Memories | 95 |
| 18 | Tukituki | 99 |
| 19 | Delusion | 102 |
| 20 | Empathy | 105 |
| 21 | Farewell | 109 |
| 22 | Ramblings | 113 |
| 23 | A gathering | 116 |
| 24 | Passion | 123 |
| 25 | Death | 128 |
| 26 | Jubilee | 133 |
| 27 | Remember | 137 |

*To Joan Watters, Ella, Sophie, Sam,
and in memory of Joan Harvey*

For me this is an unusual book for it is a departure from my usual style of writing. It is set mainly in New Zealand, a country that I have visited many times and have grown to love for its tranquillity and natural beauty. Having said that, the location might well be anywhere in this world for it simply provides the vehicle for an inner journey which I have attempted to express in a concise prose style.

The result is not a 'tidy' book for there is a certain amount of rambling within its pages. That is how I have found my mind works, as I have attempted to record something of the different inner pathways that I have trodden across the years.

None of the prose poems in this book has been published until now but several have been read in public and have evoked an enthusiastic response from many listeners. How they will be received by the reader I know not. All I can hope for is that they may evoke a response that will encourage some readers to reflect on their own inner journey and in so doing benefit from that reflection.

There are many people to whom I am indebted for this book. First, Jenny and Alan Coles, who were generous always with their hospitality and kindly invited me to both their home in Cornwall when I needed time to write, and to share the holiday house they were renting in Hawke's Bay, New Zealand.

Jenny must have a special mention as without her encouragement and support these poems would never have seen the light of day. I would frequently write something on scraps of paper, or emails, and she would collect and save them as she was always convinced that they ought to be published. She typed and re-typed and never seemed to lose patience. The sketches throughout the book are also her work.

Sarah, my long-suffering secretary, dealt expertly with the myriad of requests and invitations that came to me when I was away for longish periods of time in New Zealand or elsewhere. I could not have managed all my other responsibilities without her help.

Frances, my wife, has accommodated herself to my frequent absences, which have been the pattern across a lifetime. I remain grateful to her for her patience and forbearing.

I remain deeply indebted to my good friend, Linda Brockbank, who spent many hours reading the manuscript and made many helpful suggestions regarding its design which eventually led to its publication. Our thanks must also go to Philip Law and the staff of SPCK for their enthusiasm.

Finally, the several individuals to whom I read an occasional poem and who were brave enough to give me an honest response – thank you all.

In the winter of 2012 I left England for New Zealand where I was to join a cruise ship in order to deliver a series of lectures. Friends suggested that I might care to fly out early and share their holiday house which they had rented in the Hawke's Bay area. They knew I wanted to write a book and said that this lovely part of New Zealand would be an ideal place in which to start work. I did and thus this book was born.

Over 20 years previously, when held in solitary confinement as a hostage, I had written a book in my head, *Taken on Trust*. It was written in that way as I was not allowed pencil and paper and thus it was the only way possible I could manage to write. Years later I committed it to paper at Trinity Hall, Cambridge. I had also written novels and scraps of poetry in the same way but they have long since been lost to memory.

For those readers unfamiliar with the story suffice to say that as a member of Archbishop Robert Runcie's staff I had engaged in successful negotiations for the release of hostages in Iran and Libya. In the mid-1980s, when hostage-taking was rife in Beirut, I was at first asked to be involved in seeking the release of two American clerics who had been kidnapped there. Later, I was asked by relatives to try and do something for British hostages.

Quite frankly, it was with some reluctance that I took up these cases. Alas, I fell victim to political duplicity which went by the name of Iran-Contra. This matter has been well documented elsewhere and this is not the place for me to go into lengthy explanations. I refused to let go of the hostages after I had established face-to-face contact with their kidnappers, and when I received a promise of safe conduct to actually visit the imprisoned men, whose health was said to be failing, I accepted knowing in my heart the acute risk I was taking. Robert was reluctant to let me return to Beirut at a time when there had been the political collapse occasioned by the Contra affair and I fully appreciated his reluctance. I would have said exactly what he said had a member of my staff wanted to continue under such adverse circumstances. However, he finally agreed to my return and I went back. The kidnappers broke their word to me which, frankly, did not come as a great surprise and I spent almost five years in captivity. I do not in any way regret taking that decision for myself, but I do regret the anguish it caused both to my family and to Robert and his wife.

I have hazy recollections of my return to the UK after spending so many years incarcerated in Beirut. It was not all plain sailing. Some in the media accused me of being deeply implicated in the Iran-Contra arms-dealing scandal when the truth was that I knew absolutely nothing at all about that matter. Others claimed that I thought myself to be invincible because I believed God would protect me from being captured! Nothing could be further from the truth. I have never believed that, because one has a faith, then one is given 'super protection' from the normal ups and downs of life. Such comments disturb me not at all now, but then, when I was feeling vulnerable and having to face the task of returning to a world that had changed in so many respects from the world I knew previously, they hurt me deeply.

I gave an extempore address after landing at RAF Lyneham. After delivering it I gave no further interviews for over a year.

Introduction

Apart from a brief verse printed in my school magazine over 60 years ago I have never published or written poetry, but as the years went by I decided that I ought to try writing myself in order to give expression to feelings and emotions common to all human beings, and also to try and describe concisely some of the events that have occupied my time since my release years ago. I wrote a considerable number. Some I shared with friends and one or two I read during the course of lectures I was giving. To my surprise they received a very positive response and I was urged to publish.

I was, and to a degree still am, somewhat reluctant to share them with a wider audience but eventually decided I would give it a try. Rather than simply publish the poems by themselves, I chose to use them to illustrate a narrative which describes something of the rambling pathway I have taken through life.

This collection, the compilation of which started in New Zealand and was completed in Cornwall, is now placed before you, the reader. As I do so I can't help but remember the admonition of Oscar Wilde when he is reputed to have said, 'All bad poetry springs from genuine feelings.' However, it is my hope that the poems printed here may resonate with you as you also tread the winding and mysterious pathway through life. You will, of course, have your individual interpretation of this book and will conjure up your own pictures of what I am trying to convey. For what they are worth, I place these words before you and in so doing place a part of my life in your hands.

It is a warm sunny day as I sit down to write. Several days ago, on a cold damp December evening, I left Heathrow Airport in London bound for Auckland, New Zealand. Now I am in a beautiful rural location surrounded by open countryside. The house, which is spacious and cool, is set at the top of a small hill. Below, one may catch sight of the Tukituki river as it meanders its way to the sea some 20 miles distant. A small farmstead lies at the foot of the hill. Occasionally someone may walk from the farm across the pasture, but throughout the day that is the only human being one may see. It is the perfect place from which to look back across the years and to reflect on events that took place long ago and that have subsequently shaped my life.

*Memories, Dreams, Reflections.* It was the Swiss psychotherapist Carl Jung who took these three words for the title of his autobiography and to me they encapsulate what I intend this book to be. I shall not necessarily follow a chronological order in my writing. Dreams and memories which occasion reflection do not work in such a way. A dream will be experienced and then vanish as quickly as it appeared. Some will linger for many a year. Memories swirl around in the mind and as the years pass by are often distorted as though, from the unconscious, one is attempting to make them acceptable. Some refuse to change and remain to give rise to a range of conflicting emotions.

As I prepared to write this first chapter I happened by chance to come across the writings of the late Philip Rieff, one of the leading interpreters of Freud. He wrote that desire and limitation, eros and authority are intimately connected. The tension between them provides the energy for all artistic endeavours. These two sentences struck home as they put into a nutshell something of my own experience. Through the poems I have attempted to give some expression to the range of conflicting emotions that are within me, as they are within all people. On the one hand there is the limitation and authority which I have accepted because of my whole upbringing, particularly having been brought up by a very strict father. On the other there are the human emotions equally strong. It is only now, in the latter years of mortal life, that I have been able to give some expression to these powerful forces through poetic writing.

The following lines, written long before I read Rieff, followed a lengthy discussion with a close friend and partially explain why his writings so impressed me. In the discussion we had I was attempting to understand why I had the desire to express myself in what was a different way of writing for me.

The following poem may seem unduly morose to some, but the fact is that I *am* in the final quarter of life and now is the time for me to reflect on what has been, what is and what hopefully will be.

## SELF EXAMINATION

Can it be
That this sudden burst
Of poetic activity
Long held back
By fear,
Or doubt:
Can it be that this is a precursor
Of a mortal life rapidly drawing to a close?
The words stream forth
Filling the page with hopes,
Desires,
They rush to find a place,
Knowing that their source
Will soon be no more;
Himself a word, a memory,
Incapable of creating,
Incapable of loving, holding, caring,
A memory;
A memory of one who tried to love,
Who needed love;
A memory of one admired by some
Who knew not his inner pain,
His inner striving for wholeness,
His deep inner conflict
With light and darkness.
'A religious man' some said.
They knew nothing.
Nothing of his inner agony.
Nothing of his agony of disbelief,
Nothing of his striving to find truth,

Nothing of his desire to live truth
And so often failing.
'A worthy man' some said.
They knew nothing of his rejection of acclaim
And his desire for it.
A desire to be known, respected
And yet
It was simply a desire to be loved.
In the past days the flood gates of emotion
Have been opened.
Now, in these last days, they are
Thrown wide.
Secretly.
Privately
There is still a deep inner terror
That love and passion will destroy
An edifice created across life.
The days shorten
And life moves on its relentless way.
I give these words to you my friend.
Guard them,
Protect them:
They are my impoverished soul,
The soul that you know
And have loved.

It is evening and I am sitting on a small veranda overlooking the farmstead at the foot of the hill. My two friends, husband and wife, with whom I am sharing this house, have left for an evening stroll, leaving me to my thoughts. The sun is gradually setting, filling the sky with a blaze of colour. There is a slight breeze. In the hilly meadow two longhorn cattle, Buster and Dudley, gaze curiously at me as I write. We are told that they are especially fond of apples and carrots and will come to receive these titbits from those who stay in the house. The cattle belong to the owners of this property and are kept as pets. In the distance sheep graze. It is often said that New Zealand resembles England as it was 30 or 40 years ago and there is a certain truth in that statement. The population is tiny, approximately four and a half million throughout the North and South Islands. Consequently the roads are relatively empty of traffic and life has a certain tranquillity that has been lost in many parts of the British Isles.

As I sit in the calm of the evening I am reminded yet again that I am in the final stage of mortal life. I don't feel in any way morbid about this, simply grateful that I am in good health and able to enjoy these latter years. Across the years I have brushed with death many times and in the years spent as a captive it was my daily companion. I cannot say that I was, or am, afraid of death for it is inevitable and a part of life itself. We die and the atoms that constitute our body are redistributed throughout the universe from whence we came. Ashes to ashes. Dust to dust. In captivity

I was afraid of the way in which I might die. On one occasion, when I was facing a mock execution and a gun was placed against my temple, my fear was of pain. Would it hurt when the bullet went through my brain? Today that fear belongs to the past and is simply a memory. Towards the end of captivity my health almost gave out when I developed a severe bronchial infection. I could not lie down for weeks and slept sitting on the floor with my back propped against the wall. As there was no medical attention whatsoever it took considerable effort to hold on to life. The intense loneliness of the experience, when I needed the care and support of another human being, is reflected in the following poem.

Buster and Dudley

## ALONE

Alone,
Day follows day
With relentless monotony.
My body is wearing away.
Each hour I hold to life,
With failing strength.
My body is failing.

Year after year
I have clutched at life
As a drowning man
Would hold to a straw.
Now I see the spectre of death.
It hovers around
Taunting, mocking.
My strength ebbs away,
Ebbs from the shores of life,
Leaving me without breath.
I will not die,
Will not.
Will not . . .

Now I am lost,
Lost in the world of fitful sleep;
Respite,
Blessed respite.
Release from chains,
From beatings,
From the spectre that haunts.
I wake,
My back against the wall.
I cannot lie for I will choke,

My breath is leaving me,
Leaving.

My darling,
In those dark days
Where were you?
Were you with me in spirit?
Were you with me
In the world where the living
And the dead
Walk together,
Conscious
And unconscious?
Today you hold my bruised soul
Tenderly, lovingly.
I ask no sympathy,
No tears;
I hardly ask for that
Which you have given so freely,
Your love.

You were with me,
You were and are,
For we live in time
And beyond time.
Life is a true mystery
And we walk together
Along its corridors.
One day we shall step beyond time
Into that realm I have touched.
Death is but a gateway
Through which we pass alone;
But those who know love,
Before that last mortal journey,
Have known life:
Have found the secret of immortality.

In many of my musings I walked with different companions.
Sometimes, like Dante, I would conjure up a Beatrice figure. At
other times I would seek the companionship of those with whom
I had shared something of my life in the past. Naturally I was lonely,
but when illness struck I discovered a new depth in that experience.
Up to that point I had been able to combat loneliness by using my
imagination to talk and share with those whom I had known in
freedom. Now, when illness struck, I said to myself that death would
be preferable to what I felt was becoming a living death. Yet somehow
I found the strength to fight on. I did not want my family and friends
not to know how I had lived my final days on earth. If I were to die in
captivity they would always have to live with that awful 'not knowing'.

Throughout my life I have had contact with many hostages and
their families and because of my own experience have gained an
understanding of the agonies they experience when nothing more is
heard from the person for whom they care. Somehow, despite the
illness, I found the strength to continue to battle and not to succumb.

## DREAMS

In years spent alone
I lived from within.
Awake and asleep
I walked the land of
Dreams,
Memories,
Reflections.

Chains held my body,
Eyes cloaked from human encounter,
I retreated within.
No chains held my dreams.
I saw the blue, blue sky,
The raging ocean.
I crossed the parched desert.

No boundary
In the world of dream,
No crying for freedom.
Liberty,
Boundless liberty
Was mine
In this open land of dreams.

Freedom was in dream.
In memory new chains held,
Self-imposed chains,
Chains to prevent hurt.
I saw my family,
My friends,
Those whom I loved.
Consciously I let them fade
To ease the pain of separation.

Do I still live from deep within?
Does the wall,
Erected by my captors,
Remain?
Now I may touch another,
Feel the wind
On my face,
The earth
Beneath my feet;
Now I walk freely,
With care.
Deep within
There is a private place,
Open only to the ones I love
And trust.
Self-imposed chains;
The key is yours, my love.
The key is yours.

Once, when I was so ill that I lapsed into unconsciousness, my captors moved me into a room and sat me before an open window. I remained chained and blindfolded, but for the first time in years I could feel the gentle wind on my face and the healing warmth of the sun. It was an experience that I shall never forget. Alas, after half an hour or so I was returned to my dark cell and the favour was never repeated. Now, on a warm evening when the sun is gradually sinking in the sky and the wind gently murmurs around the house, I recognize once again how precious freedom is.

It is only recently that, by writing poetry, I have allowed others than those very close to me to enter my private inner space and I do so in this book. Most people, wisely perhaps, keep many of their doubts and conflicts hidden for fear of being ridiculed and thus hurt. The truth is that we are all, to a certain extent, riddled with conflicting inner forces. The loneliness I experienced for much of my life, and that I experienced significantly in the latter months of captivity, has now diminished considerably. I have come to realize that loneliness is predominately a state of mind and not necessarily an absence of human companionship. Today, in freedom, I seek time alone and value it. The fact that I can be alone enables me to be more fully with others when I am in their company. One of the gifts I received from the years of incarceration is to be able to embrace solitude as a friend, and in that embrace enjoy the calm that it brings. In this solitary place in New Zealand my inner solitude is united with the solitude around me and that, in itself, is a healing experience.

## 3 Dawn

This morning I woke as dawn was breaking. From my bedroom window there is the most lovely view of the meadow where Dudley and Buster graze contentedly. I stepped outside into the clean, cool morning air. Within a few moments the heat from the sun would dry the dew that had collected on the veranda table, where later we would have breakfast. In the middle distance the river caught the beams of the morning sun and responded with a sparkle. One could not help but feel what a wonderful world this is, despite the triteness of that saying.

Back indoors I sit at the long dining table and prepare to write before my companions in the house stir. We are but a few days into the new year of 2012. I saw the new year in on a British Airways flight as we flew over Prague en route to Bangkok. The sky was clear and looking down one could see thousands of coloured lights from bonfires and fireworks lit to celebrate the occasion. Now my thoughts return to the old year and some of the events that have remained in my mind.

I continue to be appalled that the Guantanamo situation is not yet finally resolved. The fact that nations which regard themselves as civilized and respecters of the rule of law could, and did, engage in torture of those suspected of involvement in terrorist activities is truly shameful. Respect for human dignity has always been a precious and scarce commodity, but in the past year it suffered major assaults. Iran, Israel, Palestine, Zimbabwe: there is little need for me to go into detail for in all those locations, as well as in many others around the world, individuals have suffered humiliation and torture. In certain cases torture has been sanctioned by the state, which has concocted clever legal arguments to justify inhuman practices.

As I sit on the veranda and watch the sun slowly rise I reflect on the beauty surrounding me. But the conflicts that exist deep within myself and within all human beings are also rampant across the world. In this poem I wrote about my own experience of torture.

## FOOTSTEPS IN THE CORRIDOR

They came
At night.
Footsteps in the corridor,
A key turning
As fear grips my stomach.
I lie still on the floor,
Blindfolded,
Sheltering beneath
My thin blanket,
Seeking protection,
Seeking what scrap of security
I may find.

'Sit!'
The command echoes round the cell
Like a shot from a pistol.
Chains tug at my limbs
As I struggle to obey.
My wrists and feet are seized
As locks are removed.

'Stand.'
I stumble to my feet,

What is happening?
Why at this hour do they come?
Can this be release?
Do I stand on the brink of freedom?
My arms are gripped
As we move out of the cell
Into the unknown.

There are many in the room.
I hear laughter,
Words uttered in a half whisper,
Words I cannot understand.
'Sit!'
I crouch and sit.
'Sleep.'
I lie on my back;
The room falls silent.
'What you say?'
Now I understand.
Another interrogation,
Another bout of questioning,
Another seeking for answers
I cannot give.
'What you say?'
The voice is louder,
Insistent.
'Nothing,' I reply, 'Nothing.'
Something lands on my face,
A pillow perhaps?
I struggle to breathe
As the pillow is held down.

'What you say?'
Someone holds my legs,

Now my fear increases.
The room falls silent.
Suddenly,
A searing pain
Convulses my body,
My feet are burning
As blow after blow is struck
With cable.
'What you say?'
'What you say?'
I cry into the covering.
'O God. Let this pain cease.'
What manner of person
Can so treat another human being
To such indignity
And pain?
'Stand.'
I cannot.
Arms lift me to my feet
And drag me back into chains;
Back into the night,
Back into a living death.

When I was dragged back into my cell and the shackles were replaced around my hands and feet, I lay for a while in shock. I felt an overwhelming sense of pity for the one who had administered the beating. How could he bring himself to treat another human being in such a way? How could torturers the world over bring themselves to engage in such degrading practices? Thank God for Amnesty International and Human Rights Watch for their constant vigilance and protestations against inhuman treatment, no matter where it might occur or by whom it is administered.

# 4 Justice

Being in New Zealand for a few weeks, one is well ahead of the UK timewise. There is a 13-hour time difference in their summer and on the journey out one loses a whole day. Initially it's confusing, but simple enough once one gets accustomed to it. I usually write in the early morning when darkness has fallen in Britain. It is then that I often look at emails. Today as I return to writing, following my poem about torture, my peace has been disturbed by an email from a colleague detailing the latest situation facing a prisoner in a British jail whom we have both been supporting for a long time. The prisoner is currently serving a life sentence for murder and within a few weeks will come before the Parole Board, who will consider whether or not the prisoner is suitable for release on licence. Board members are faced with an unenviable task for if they make one mistake they are sure to be pilloried by the media and, of course, the consequences can be tragic if there are further victims.

My own involvement with prisons and the criminal justice system in the UK goes back many years. Over 20 years ago I was one of the founder members of the Butler Trust, an organization set up in the early 1980s in memory of the late R. A. Butler, a former Home Secretary, to give public recognition to those men and women who are doing commendable work within the prison system. There are many such men and women who, day in and day out, work with prisoners, many of whom are mentally unstable or who suffer from various personality disorders. The email I received today alleges that the prisoner we are supporting has been subject to various forms of intimidation by some prison staff, and regrettably such behaviour is not unknown but is exceptionally difficult to prove. Some prison staff who may have come from fairly routine occupations now find themselves in a position where they have considerable power over the lives of others. The consequences for a prisoner to whom they have taken a dislike can be disastrous.

During the course of a year I receive many letters from prisoners claiming that they have been wrongly convicted and asking if I can assist them. Again, this faces me with a task that is virtually impossible. I know that not all who write can be innocent, although many prisoners convince themselves that they are. I also know that from time to time innocent people do get convicted and sent down for a long sentence. The fact is that once an individual gets caught in the criminal justice system it is the devil's own job to get free!

Although I have been associated with prisons and prisoners for over 50 years, my own captivity has enabled me to understand more fully what it is like to be totally at the mercy of others. It is so often said, mainly by those who have little or no knowledge of prison life, that UK prisons are too easy. Many who make such assertions hardly know what it is like to lose freedom; to have all movements monitored; to have little or no privacy; to be virtually powerless when there is a family crisis. All the above and more add up to real punishment. Prisons are also supposed to be places where individuals are given an opportunity to face their offending behaviour and be equipped to return to mainstream life. Many do get such assistance, but there are substantial numbers who do not. An individual prison may rehabilitate a prisoner who has a serious addiction problem, but a new problem comes when the prisoner leaves jail. There is much work to be done in assisting people back into mainstream life once they have completed their sentence. Short sentences are virtually useless and properly supervised restorative justice programmes are certainly part of the way forward. The key words there are 'properly supervised'.

One ought not to forget the victims of crime. Some years ago I met a young man who had suffered a terrible tragedy when his family were caught in the midst of a civil war. One day armed men entered the room in which his family was gathered and shot and killed everyone in sight. He hid under a table and thus escaped with his life. Owing to the trauma he had suffered he could not speak and it was a considerable time before he began to function normally, thanks to the help of a specialized team trained in dealing with such conditions.

This event took place overseas but every day, somewhere in the British Isles, there are new victims of murder or other crimes. The effect of that crime on the victim can be dreadful and a part of a good restorative justice programme is to bring the perpetrator of the crime face to face with the victim, so that the perpetrator may understand the effect his or her action has had on that person. This procedure is not appropriate in every situation but does work extremely well where it is followed correctly.

Tim Newell, who for many years was a prison governor and is now in his retirement, runs an organization called Escaping Victimhood. This group works especially with those unfortunate individuals who have experienced a murder and gives them the support so necessary if they are to continue to lead a normal life.

For some prisoners, time spent locked up can provide them with an opportunity for introspective reflection, and this can be painful. I wrote the following poem when I felt the terror of being deeply alone in a vast universe and when I felt the need for human companionship and for the assurance that religious belief brings to some. I did not feel the close presence of God but nevertheless I cried out . . .

## AT NIGHT

In the silent recesses of night
All without is still.
The fever of life is over,
The busy world is hushed.
In the silent recesses of night
All is still.

In the silent recesses of night
My eyes close.
Fever over,
World hushed.
Deep within,
In the dark recesses of soul,
Fever rages.

Be still my soul,
Be still.
Be at one with your creator,
Healer,
Father,
Mother,
Giver of life.

In the silent recesses of night,
Across the ocean of dreams,
Fear stalks my soul.
The waters are deep;
There is no chart.
In feverish haste I reach out;
Hold me,
Hold me,
Then I shall be still.

In the silent recesses of night
I sleep.
The ocean calms,
Stillness enters my soul.
Stillness within,
Stillness without,
A restless stillness.

In the silent recesses of night
I sleep alone.
Alone on the ocean,
Longing to be held,
Longing to be safe,
Longing to be healed.
The fever of life is over.
The busy world is hushed.
I rest in my creator,
But for a moment.
Heal me O God.
Without you I drown.

Dartmoor Prison is not the oldest prison in the UK in use today. That dubious distinction belongs to HMP Shepton Mallet, which has been in continuous use since the seventeenth century but is now faced with closure.* Dartmoor, however, is a name that resonates with many people in the British Isles, and although it is (at the time of writing) no longer a maximum security prison, the past still lingers and, because of its location in a valley on the moors, it really does seem to get more than its fair share of bad weather.

-----

* Shepton Mallet Prison closed 27 March 2013.

It is not generally known that it was built to house prisoners taken during the Napoleonic wars and later housed prisoners captured during the American War of Independence. There is a small plot, adjacent to the prison, where some of these prisoners are buried, and from time to time Daughters of the American Revolution come over from the United States and hold a simple service of remembrance for those long dead.

I have visited Dartmoor many times for, despite the grim surroundings, it is the centre of one of the most creative schemes, run by volunteers, within the prison system. One of the many problems facing prisoners who have a family is how to keep the family together and especially how to see that children get adequate support. Storybook is a project developed by Sharon Berry, and run by a team of dedicated staff and volunteers, which enables prisoners to record a bedtime story on CD or DVD. The story is then animated by a trained team of prisoners and the product sent to the prisoner's family. One prisoner, who was totally illiterate, repeated the sentences given to him by a reader and these were recorded, animated and sent to his children. When he heard the finished recording he wept. 'I have never been able to do anything like that for my children,' he said.

Although the prison has a grim history shown in part in the following brief extract from a history of the prison and in a poem I wrote, it has become a creative centre within the justice system and Storybook is now operative in over 100 prisons throughout the British Isles. I am proud to be their patron.

### The massacre of American prisoners

Captain Shortland went at the head of the soldiers and ordered all of the prisoners back. They refused and, as the bread wagon was at this moment making a delivery to the stores, there was a fear that the prisoners might attempt to take control. Again the order was given to return while the soldiers fixed bayonets and began to advance. They were about three paces from the prisoners but still the Americans stood firm and refused to back down. The order to charge was given and the prisoners instantly broke and ran as fast as possible to the safety of their prisons. There were thousands of Americans desperately trying to get back into the buildings but they could not do so quickly. The order to fire was given, there is some doubt as to who by, but the Americans later insisted that it was Captain Shortland. The soldiers obeyed and fired a full volley. The volleys were repeated for several rounds with prisoners falling dead and wounded all around.

(An extract from Ron Joy, *Dartmoor Prison: A Complete Illustrated History: The World's Most Famous Prison*, Wellington, Somerset: Halsgrove, 2002)

Dartmoor Prison

## DARTMOOR

The grey deep mist
Lay silently
Across the valley.
Penetrating dampness
Chilled the bones
And made one long
For warmer climes.

Princeton,
A poor scrap of a town,
Lay shivering
Under a blanket
Of icy gloom,
Longing to be embraced

By a warmth
Yet several months
Hence.

Through this very street
Along which we drove,
Soldiers of Napoleon
Shuffled in chains.
Captives from the New World
Joined this dreary train,
Many destined
Never to return to their homeland,
Their ghostly presence
Lingering deep in the valley.
William Adam,
Peter Birch,
John Collins,
James Hart,
Placid Lovely,
John Williams.
They and others
Sleep
With their companions.
Unmarked by stone or cross,
Remembered only in archives.

A white vehicle passes silently,
Headlights barely penetrating
The all enveloping cloak.
Within, a new generation
Of captives sit tightly
In their cubicles,
Waiting.

Listening for the slightest sound
Of a freedom they once knew.
Will they leave here?
Will the damp so grip their bones
That their lives are extinguished
And they too are lost
In the mists of time?

The white mist
Cloaks all in silence
As the van
Fades from sight
Through the protective gate.
We are left with our thoughts.
The ghosts of yesteryear
Wait silently
To greet their new companions.
Gently
And quietly
Pale straws of sunlight
Seek entry
Through the mist.

# 5 Moods

For the past 18 hours it has rained incessantly here in Hawke's Bay. The hills surrounding the house have been shrouded with a grey mist and this morning, when the river is once again visible, one may see that it has vastly increased in size, flooding the pastures on each bank. The change from bright clear skies to impenetrable mist, from a gentle waterway to a raging torrent, has been instant and dramatic. Moods and feelings can and do change at the same speed. At one moment one may feel peace and contentment and in an instant the mood can change and one is lost in the darkness that exists within.

One of the ways in which I survived in captivity was by taking an interior journey. The danger of such an approach is that as one travels alone through the recesses of the mind one encounters both light and darkness. Memories that are both pleasant and supportive are resurrected along with memories that disturb. Throughout, one is attempting to find inner balance, inner harmony.

## CAPTIVE THOUGHTS

I walk the corridor of my mind
With hesitant steps.
I see a thousand faces
That tell a thousand stories.
I have walked with them,
Laughed with them,
Cried with them,
Nurtured them;
Sometimes I have fought with them.
I see a face, creased and worn

With the ravages of time;
You nurtured me,
You gave me life,
Now, far along the corridor,
I see you,
My father,
Long passed from mortal life,
But alive in this hidden place.

I am alone,
But the corridor is full.
I see you,
My mother;
How you tried to love me,
To embrace me,
I stood alone,
A small child,
Afraid that I would be lost,
Abandoned,
Afraid that love would trap me
Like a bird in a snare;
I long to be loved.

I walk the corridor of my mind.
I see you,
My friend.
Were you always there?
Why did you suddenly appear
In the latter days of mortal life?
Chance? Design?
You see me.
You know me.
You say you love me.
And I weep like the child I am,
And always have been.

This evening, in search of some exercise, we drove the ten or so miles to Kairakau Beach, a small seaside settlement. To get there we crossed the single-track road bridge spanning the River Tukituki. This is a Maori name derived from the sound made when the sand is patted with the flat of the hand by those who are looking for eels. We drove on for several miles until we could go no further without dropping into the sea where a small river, the Mangakuri, ends its short life. The whole ocean front was strewn with thousands of branches and logs of all shapes and sizes, many of which had been deposited on the shore from the river following the recent heavy rains. Back at the house the rain has produced a carpet of small yellow flowers that cover the meadow and contrast against the lush green of the grassland. Although this is midsummer in New Zealand, far from being burnt and brown the hills have been refreshed by the rains of recent days. I loved this house and surroundings from the first moment we stepped over the threshold and my delight increases as the days go by.

Although we are in the heart of the countryside a drive of seven or eight miles will get us to a shop in Waipawa where we can buy basic foodstuffs and a little further down the road, in Waipukurau, everything we need is readily available. Passing through Waipawa no one could help but notice a small wooden building proudly signed 'The Clock Shop'. As a lover of clocks of all descriptions I could not pass without taking a quick look inside and was not disappointed. There, arrayed around the room, were clocks ancient and modern of all descriptions. Cuckoo clocks, long case clocks, modern clocks made in China, antique Ansonia railway clocks made in the USA. It was a timekeeper's paradise.

The owner and his wife greeted us warmly and before too much time had passed we had been invited to go round to their house for tea before we left New Zealand. I needed a new, extra large strap for my wristwatch which they did not have in stock, but they amazed me by saying that they could get it for me in 24 hours!

Back home there was an email from Belfast, a city I know well as I was married there and my mother-in-law, who is 102, continues to live there alone in her own house. She still attends at least two educational classes a week, one of which is lip-reading as she says she might need it one day!

Naturally there was a great family party to celebrate the hundredth birthday and friends and relatives from across the world gathered to mark this momentous occasion. I wrote the following lines for my mother-in-law, Joan Watters.

One explanation is required. My father-in-law, Joan's husband of course, was a solicitor, thus the line, 'Gave himself to law'.

## A DYING EMPIRE*

Straw boaters,
Striped blazers,
Ladies with long skirts
Gracefully carried on a bicycle.
Long hot summer days
When all was tranquil,
When champagne cooled
By the river bank,
When sun never cast a shadow
Over Empire.
Edwardian days,
Days of your infancy Joan,
Days when with your first breath
You inhaled the aroma
Of power
And privilege,
So ably won
By your forefathers.

Who was to know
That Empire was fading,
That boaters would give way
To iron helmets,
That those who

---

* Dedicated to Joan Watters.

Gracefully travelled
The towpath
Would now roll bandages
For their wounded lovers?

Who was to know
That in your infancy
A mighty war would rage,
Shattering dreams,
Filling the earth
With a million screams,
As limb was torn from limb?
The bicycle,
Now no more,
Transformed
Into a tangled web
Of wire,
Impeding the enemy,
And tearing at those
Who would seek free passage.

Who was to know,
That promise of war
To end all war
Was but empty rhetoric?
We may hope,
We may wish
For flowers to bloom
From the ravages of war.
A million flowers bloom,
Alas, poppies,
Blood red,
Deep blood red;

They do not wilt
In the heat of summer.
Their life has gone
As you begin yours.

Who was to know,
When you were young,
Living with a fragile peace,
That far away
In a place
Built to supply Empire,
Your future partner
Gave himself to law,
And then to you.
Days long ago,
White gowns,
Dark suits,
Pious sentiments,
A home in Belfast.

We all know
That peace must be guarded,
That power seeks to multiply
And smash
All who would impede
Its quest.
We look across the fields of Flanders,
Another million poppies,
Shattered dreams,
Your own brother among them.
Edwardian days
Are but a memory;
Empire is dying.

Apart from family ties, Northern Ireland has played a significant role in my life as I have been involved with many efforts across the years to promote peace throughout the community. As a patron of the Warrington Male Voice Choir I made many visits with them as they brought different groups together using music to promote harmony and understanding. In Omagh, scene of the terrible bombing incident which killed and maimed so many innocent people, I have worked with those who suffered, and in some cases continue to suffer, the trauma brought about by this event. A friend of mine, Michael, now works full time with individuals who continue to bear the psychological scars of violence. His story typifies the courage and resilience of so many people from Northern Ireland. As a police officer he was travelling on patrol in a Land Rover when a missile was fired through the cab and removed both of his hands. Eventually help got to him and he began the long process of rehabilitation. Following lengthy and repeated surgery he had a fixed hand fitted on one arm and a mechanical hand on the other. He then gained admittance to university where he worked for a first degree. He now has two doctoral degrees and an OBE for services to health care in Northern Ireland and is busy working as a clinical psychologist in Belfast. Like many others he had the strength of character to turn tragedy around. Alas, there are many who are not so fortunate and have had their lives destroyed.

On a recent visit to the Province I sat in my room reflecting on my years spent in that country. Looking out at the green hills surrounding the city of Belfast I wrote the following:

## MY SILENT ROOM

From my silent room
I look across this sad city.
In the distance
Green hills,
Standing since time began.
Do they promise help
To a people wounded,
Destroyed by violence?
'I will lift up mine eyes
Unto the hills,'
Said the psalmist.
The hills remain motionless,
God is mute.
No voice thunders
From the mountain top,
No prophet descends.
People weep
And mourn.

In my silent room
My heart is heavy.
I think of those whom I know:
'My son was blown into pieces,'
'My wife was taken and shot.'
In my silent room
I cry,
Cry for the suffering of so many.
They looked to the hills,
Attended church,
Said their prayers;
The sentinels ringed the city
Trapping a people

In their agony;
False prophets voiced words of hate
And empty words of hope.
The hills remained silent
As death stalked the land.

From my silent room
I see the first blossoms of spring,
Shooting from a soil
Made fertile
By the blood of innocents.
'When my heart is overwhelmed,' wrote
    the psalmist,
'I look to the rock
That is higher than I.'
We have looked to the hills,
We have looked for help,
We are made deaf
With silence.
In my silent room,
Alone,
I look within.
Be calm my soul,
Listen.
The small voice speaks,
Find peace within,
Learn to love,
Let the first blossoms bloom
From your wounded soul.
The pale daffodils
Sway in the gentle breeze,
The hills are green,
New life is coming,
Be at peace.

There is a friend with whom I have worked on several occasions. She is a gentle, compassionate individual and in her quiet way has helped many deal with the terror that they have faced. I wrote the following poem as she and I returned to her family home following a day spent listening to the stories of those who had been so deeply wounded by violence.

### OMAGH

It is evening.
The light is fading
As we journey to our home
For the night.
Hidden in the fold
Of gentle hills,
Our resting place
Is waiting.
Waiting to welcome,
Waiting to offer respite
From the burdens of the day.

Not a league from this place
Blood flows through the streets.
Burning metal
Shatters a skull,
Maims a child,
Pierces a heart;
'But that was yesteryear,'
Some may say.
It was.
Alas,
Suffering is not trapped by time,

It roams freely,
Active in a realm
Where those of troubled mind
Are wounded daily,
Ever given to tasting the blood
That so cruelly
Brought them to the depths of despair.

It is night,
The light has faded
In Omagh town.
A mother,
Sleeping fitfully,
Sees her child
Walking, walking,
Ever walking.
She stretches out
To catch her boy.
He slips away
From her bloodied hand;
Her screams rend the troubled streets.
Her boy,
Free from time,
Ever imprisoned in memory.

The night is passing,
We sit before an open fire
In the deep silence
Of the house.
I listen to you my friend;
Not so much to your words,
More to your presence,
Your elegant simplicity,

Your smile,
Tinged with a sadness
That comes from touching troubled waters.
You walk the corridors of memory.
You dream,
And as you dream
The ghosts are named.
The shadows of night
Lose their terror
And gently hold you
In peace.

It is dawn
The first shafts of light
Dispel the shadows.
The spectres of night
Merge with the gentle mist of the morning.
In Omagh town
The wounded stir
From their beds.
The mother raises
Her weary head
Preparing to walk
The bloodied streets.

In the realm beyond time
We walk together,
Awake,
Asleep.
Today, my friend,
You will name your ghosts
And they will die.
The mother will flee

And they will torment
In the realm beyond time.
We stretch out a hand
To touch the wounded,
To hold a hand,
To face the spectres of night
And name them in the gentle light of dawn.

Lighten our darkness
We beseech thee O Lord,
And by thy great mercy
Defend us from all the perils of this night.

So be it.

# 7 Ageing

As I write my mother-in-law remains in astonishing good health despite her years, but there are many elderly people who are not so fortunate. As society changes and the number of older people increases, their support in latter years becomes a major issue. Even if a family wanted to incorporate an elderly relative in their immediate family circle the majority of modern homes are just not large enough for such provision.

Care homes are one option but they are extremely expensive for those who have to pay and vary considerably in quality. For those who are seriously or terminally ill hospices are a godsend. I first knew the founder of the hospice movement in the UK, Cicely Saunders, when she was a young general practitioner. Hospices have helped thousands of people to manage pain successfully and die with dignity. As a patron of the East Cheshire Hospice in Macclesfield, I continue to be amazed at the sums of money required to be raised each year to maintain the hospice and am full of admiration for those who work so creatively in such places.

The mother of one of the friends with whom I am staying at the moment is in a care home and has been for some considerable time. I visited her and wrote the following poem afterwards. The line 'Created pictures of days long past' refers to the fact that the old lady was a watercolour artist of no mean ability.

## WAITING*

We walked together
Along a corridor
Busy with the traffic
Of caring.
A carer smiles,
Her youthful face
Perpetuates a smile
Brought to this place
From an Asian shore.
She continues to smile
As, laboriously, she wheels a trolley
Along a corridor
Leading to the end of mortal life.

We enter a room
Full with those
Who sit and wait.
Waiting to be fed,
Waiting to be washed,
Waiting for the end
That will surely come,
Like a thief in the night,
Ready to rob those who wait
Of the last frail scraps
Of life on earth.

My companion,
A dutiful daughter,
Utters a cry of greeting:
'Hullo Mum!'

* Dedicated to Joan Harvey.

Two simple words
Bearing a lifetime of meaning.
The mother who cradled her child,
Who loved her child,
Who chastised her child,
Now sits mute,
Waiting,
Ever waiting.

We move to a simple room
Surrounded by the memories of a life lived.
The old lady sits mute.
'I brought a friend to see you, Mum.'
The daughter's voice,
Pitched louder than usual,
Betrays a determination
To bolster the spirit,
To remain hopeful,
To capture days that have long passed.
Now in the last years
The old lady sits mute,
Waiting,
Ever waiting.

I take a thin warm hand in mine,
The hand that cradled the child,
The hand that with consummate skill
Created pictures of days long past.
Now this hand rests in mine.
We remain silent.
I look into the deep pools of her eyes,
Puzzled,
Yet touched with a sparkle

That shines from the past.
Country holidays,
Schooldays,
Deep in the eyes
I see those days
Caught in a glance,
Caught in the silence.

I watch the daughter
Move quickly through the room
Straightening a crumpled bed,
Examining a record book,
Spoon-feeding her mother
As once the mother nourished her.
Now the child
Is the mother;
The mother is the child.
Life has completed its circle.

We say goodbye,
Goodbye to a worn frail body,
Home for yet a space
For a spirit
Due to leave this world.
Now we are silent together,
Remembering we are all as dust
And to dust we shall return.
Only the spirit gives life;
God grant us life
While we still have earthly time.

Today news reached us of a disaster involving a cruise ship off the coast of Italy. A quick search of the internet revealed that one of the very large ships sailing under the Costa line, and part of the huge Carnival Group, had struck a rock and capsized. There was a dramatic picture of the *Costa Concordia* lying on her side in relatively shallow water. Having lectured on board many cruise ships over the past 30 years or more this news was of considerable interest to me. In recent years cruise liners have been built to accommodate more and more people and are virtually vast floating cities. My preference is for much smaller ships and, with the exception of one or two cruise lines, I avoid these massive new monstrosities.

Not too long ago I was lecturing on a ship sailing from Australia through to New Zealand and beyond. We docked at a small port I had never heard of before, Lyttelton. This once was a thriving commercial port and is the gateway to Christchurch, some few miles away by road. Little did I know when I wrote the following lines that, within a few days of my leaving Lyttelton, disaster would strike this small community.

### LYTTELTON

Green hills
Give backdrop
To this run down, ramshackle backwater.
From aloft
Residents gaze out to sea,
Down to the once thriving harbour,
Along the tracks

Where logs are neatly stacked,
Awaiting dispatch to foreign parts.

A flyblown window space
Displays relics of Empire:
'God Save The Queen'
Emblazoned boldly on cheap cotton,
A red, white and blue waste basket,
A regal plate
Awaiting display
In some loyalist home.

Along the broken pavement
A young girl skips homeward.
Her bare, bronzed feet
Move with the lightness
Of a young gazelle.

I walk the streets
Not knowing that you were here my friend.
You drank and laughed
And then you went away.
Now I am here alone,
Gazing out to sea,
Wondering, hoping
That one day we may drink and laugh
      together
In this poor forgotten backwater,
Outpost of a once mighty Empire.

The above poem was written in February 2011. Then, as the poem
indicates, I walked around Lyttelton and went on to Christchurch.
A few days after sailing away a mighty earthquake measuring 6.3 on
the Richter scale struck the area, the epicentre of which was effectively

in Lyttelton. Christchurch Cathedral, a lovely building in which I sat for half an hour or so, was destroyed, having survived an earlier larger earthquake measuring 7.1. Many Victorian heritage buildings in Lyttelton were razed to the ground. Before coming to this house where I am now writing, I visited Christchurch again.

I travelled by ferry from Wellington to Picton through the Marlborough Sounds, which is one of the many picturesque sea journeys one may take in New Zealand. It was a calm crossing through a stretch of water that can be exceptionally turbulent at times. From Picton I drove to the seaside town of Akaroa and then from a base there visited both Lyttelton and Christchurch once again.

This time the Cathedral Square in Christchurch was sealed off from the public. What was once a thriving centre was now a ghost town. There was an eerie feeling about the place which was in direct contrast to that which I had experienced previously.

The centre of the city was also sealed off to the public and only workmen and emergency vehicles were permitted to enter. We peered through the doorway of what was once a thriving cafe/bar. Glasses and a half-empty bottle of wine rested on one table and there were signs everywhere of a hasty departure. One could virtually feel an atmosphere of gloom and depression that hung over the town. Later we were told that the incidence of suicide, breakdown and depression had risen considerably. Post traumatic stress disorder had struck with a mighty blow, leaving hundreds of casualties in its wake.

It so happened that the friends I stayed with near to Christchurch had a son who owned the log business I had seen in Lyttelton. One afternoon we drove back there. I will recount that visit in a moment, but first let me share the following poem which I wrote after the

Earthquake

Lyttelton Harbour

earthquake. The story of finding a surprisingly good second-hand
bookshop in Lyttelton is totally accurate, as is finding the book which
I bought. The second half of the poem is a product of my imagination,
but strangely enough remarkably accurate in parts. The bookshop I had
visited was totally destroyed in this second earthquake.

### BOOK ENDS

I entered a darkened room
Pungent with the distinctive odour
That emanates from old books.
This room is full of books.
A dowdy, bespectacled woman
Glances at me,
And without a word
Resumes her reading.

I am amazed.
Here in this isolated outpost
Books abound.
Biographies of those long dead,
Tales of adventure,
Even the Famous Five
Wait patiently
For some parent,
Who remembers her youth,
To take them
For the delight of another generation.

Away from home,
Away from those I love,
Joy and sorrow
Cross my path.
At times
Halting my thought,
At times
Intensifying my emotions.

A book leaps out from the gloom,
*Looking for Spinoza*;
One who knew joy and sorrow
At the extremes;
One whose restless brain
Never ceased from questioning;
One who saw his dearest friend
Hacked in pieces
By a mob of crazed fanatics.
He knew joy,
He knew sorrow.

The dowdy woman lays down her book
And attends to my purchase.
Who is she?
What stories does she tell?
Is all her life lived
From off the printed page?
What does she know
Of joy and sorrow?

I leave the darkened cavern,
Not knowing that deep sorrow
Stalks the musty shelves;
That in a space of hours
The woman will run screaming
Into the street,
The Famous Five will be flung to the floor,
The dead warriors
Will lie impotent:
Only Spinoza has been saved
From another horror
By an unwitting purchaser.

The deeds of men
May be mighty:
They may win battles,
Subdue the savage,
Gain honours.
When nature strikes
Their deeds lie dormant
On a scattered page,
Blowing along a street
Ravaged by earthquake.
Today the terror

Has leapt from the page,
Seized hold of the woman,
Compelled her to flee.
Now her body,
Nourished by fables,
But unloved by another,
Is set on fire:
Fear runs through every vein.
Her books gone for ever,
Her source of life dead;
No hero left to embrace,
Only the tattered remains of a life that was.

She may dream,
A new story can be written,
A new lover may be found.
Nature destroys,
Nature nourishes,
Tomorrow is a new day.

Alan and Jenny, with whom I am sharing the holiday house in New
Zealand, have relatives close to Akaroa on the Banks Peninsula in the
South Island and they kindly invited us to stay with them for several
days. Margaret and Derek are typical of so many New Zealanders,
hospitable and very down to earth. Some years ago Margaret was
a member of Parliament and although she now no longer sits in
Parliament she continues to be active in her local community and
in national affairs.

One warm sunny afternoon we all drove into Lyttelton, the town
I had visited just before the earthquake. From the surrounding hills
one appreciates the picturesque setting of this little port. At the time
of visiting, the rebuilding of damaged and destroyed properties had

not yet begun and so the town looked down at heel. The damage caused by the earthquake was peculiar. One would see a row of small shops and then there would be a wide gap where a property had collapsed. I looked for the bookshop which had so fascinated me, but could not place it. Then I discovered that my poem had been a reasonably accurate evocation of what had happened. An enquiry revealed that the shop had indeed been destroyed. Some stock was saved and was now on sale at the back of another small business further up the street. I sat alone for a while on a low wall looking at a site now cleared of rubble where *The Relics of Empire* had been on sale. A resident told me that the owner attempted to continue her business from her home, which had also been damaged by the earthquake.

Lyttelton Timeball Station before the earthquake

Lyttelton has its own place in history. It was in the port of Lyttelton that both Amundsen and Scott chose to set their chronometers before setting sail for the Antarctic. This was done using the Lyttelton Timeball Station, which was built in 1876. Timeball stations were an important part of many ports, being a navigational aid to ships. A ship's master could correct the ship's chronometer and ensure accurate navigation as the timeball dropped at a known Greenwich time every day. The Lyttelton Timeball, weighing over 100 kilograms, dropped at 1.00 p.m. daily down a mast on top of the octagonal stone tower. The building was a significant Lyttelton landmark, but unfortunately it is another tragic victim of the earthquakes that have struck the area, and collapsed during another major aftershock that occurred in June 2011.

'Poor Lyttelton,' I thought, as I remembered my earlier visit. How sad that you should receive such a crippling blow. Today, many cruise ships bypass the port and anchor off Akaroa some miles down the coast.

No matter which direction one looks, north, south, east or west, the views from this house where I am staying in Hawke's Bay are superb. The Tukituki, which just a few days ago was swollen, has now reverted to its normal size but remains as attractive as ever. Yesterday I watched as a Maori family swam in the slow-moving current and their black labrador splashed contentedly in and out of the water.

In the late morning we saw three or four working dogs expertly rounding up sheep in a distant meadow. The skill and speed at which this operation was performed was a joy to see. Later, we discovered that it was market day in a nearby town!

Earlier in this narrative I made mention of the fact that New Zealand reminds me of the British Isles as they were many years ago. Although in the UK we still have acres of lovely open countryside I can't help but be concerned at the way it is being eroded gradually. Some of the huge warehouses erected by the side of arterial roads are hideous and, alas, the urban sprawl on the outskirts of Christchurch, and some other New Zealand cities, is equally as terrible. I am greatly affected by the environment and without a doubt my mood is affected by the place in which I am. In the UK we have a precious asset in our countryside and it is that, as well as our historic artefacts, that attracts visitors to our shores. We are stupid in the extreme to destroy it in the name of progress. Already we have done grave damage to many towns throughout England by making one virtually indistinguishable from another.

Small local businesses ought to be encouraged by making it possible for local traders to trade through rate concessions. Street markets are a wonderful institution and really popular when they are properly run. Can it be progress to have virtually unbroken urban sprawl between Bath and Bristol? Can it be progress to allow the building of homes in green belt areas where the residents are made totally dependent on cars? As I say in the following poem, written for friends who were planting a new garden, *we* are the creators. Alas, *we* are also the destroyers, and destruction, too frequently, hides under the banner of progress.

## THE GARDEN

A lifetime flows
Like a river,
Turbulent,
Calm,
Deep and shallow.
Today the river hardly stirs.

Today,
A day when all is still,
We sit together
In an English garden.
Gone are the days
When cattle roamed
These grassy slopes.
When herdsmen
Cried their plaintive cry,
Weary with the labours
Of the day.

Today
We are calm,
As in this sheltered space,

Once wild,
Now tamed,
We rest
In the warming rays
Of a summer sun.
New seed is sown
Across the former pasture,
Transformation,
New creation,
Wrought by our hands.

The river of life
Flows gently today,
As quietly
We are transformed.
Our faces
Recording our journey,
Suffering and joy
Both sown
Deep in furrows
That line our brow.

The river of life
Flows on.
Today we rest,
Tomorrow
The ocean?
The planted seed
Stirs
In fertile soil.
Creation is one,
We are the creators.

## 10 Home

It is a common complaint, made by people of my age, that friends and acquaintances they have known for years are now increasingly occupying the pages of the obituary columns. Today news reached me of the death of Rosalind Runcie, widow of the late Robert Runcie, Archbishop of Canterbury. Lindy, as she preferred to be called by her friends, was a lively and unorthodox clergy wife. 'Too much religion makes me go pop,' she is reputed to have said, and I am sure that is what she did say. She was an accomplished musician and raised substantial sums for charity through her piano recitals.

Contrary to what many people believe, the Archbishop of Canterbury does not spend most of his time in the cathedral city. He has a home there and in my day visited Canterbury, on average, once a month. In the main the episcopal duties in the Canterbury diocese are carried out by the Bishop of Dover.

Lambeth Palace, on the bank of the Thames, has been a residence for archbishops since the thirteenth century and here in this building the archbishop of the day occupies a flat on the top floor of the main wing. Other parts of the Palace are used as offices by his small private staff. There are one or two state rooms and of course the magnificent Lambeth Palace library.

Today, as I think especially of Robert and Lindy, my mind goes back to the years I spent as a member of the Archbishop's staff at Lambeth, and I can't help but look back with gratitude for their kindness to me. Robert received such a hostile press on many an occasion, as did Lindy, and it was in those days that I learned to be careful about making judgements about people based on media reports. My captivity undoubtedly caused Robert great anguish.

When I returned from Lebanon to the UK, Robert Runcie had retired as Archbishop of Canterbury and gone to live in a modest house in St Albans, where he was once Bishop. In his retirement he supported many charities and I gave him some assistance in helping raise support for one of his favourites, a hospice in Hertfordshire. He had also become the first president of an organization that I had never heard of, named Emmaus. 'Emmaus,' he explained, 'is not a religious foundation, although it was founded in France, following the Second World War, by a remarkable French priest, the Abbé Pierre.'

The poem below is my attempt to describe how I remember the Abbé, whom I met on the final visit he made to the UK before he died.

### ABBÉ PIERRE

I see him now,
Striding forth
Along Parisian streets.
Unmistakably a cleric.
Beret,
White beard,
Cassock,
Eyes that pierced indifference
And warmed
With compassion.

No altar chained this man,
No Church controlled his life.
He was poor
With the poor,
Sad with the sad,
Hopeful with the despairing.
He walked the Parisian streets
As Christ walked to Emmaus.

The Abbé Pierre was certainly no ordinary priest. He knew his own frailties and, because of that knowledge, was able to have empathy with those who had been brought low in life. He was voted the most popular man in France year after year until finally, when he was in his nineties, he suggested that enough was enough and refused to accept further recognition. I met him just the once when he visited the UK. He was already well into his eighties and somewhat deaf. He had a reasonable command of English, far better than my schoolboy French. He died at the age of 94 in January 2007 and his funeral, in the great cathedral church of Notre Dame in Paris, was attended by both the president and prime minister of France. But those who reverently bore his body in and out of the cathedral, and who occupied a position of honour that day, were the poor and formerly destitute – the Companions, as they are known in Emmaus.

Abbé Pierre

Robert went on to tell me that Emmaus was an organization based on community principles that enabled homeless people to regain a sense of purpose in life and in many cases return to mainstream life.

'When someone enters such a community,' he said, 'they must leave behind state support, agree to work according to their capacity and leave outside the community all drink and drugs.'

Emmaus was well known in France and across the continent of Europe but totally unknown in the UK. Selwyn Image, a businessman and Cambridge resident, had seen the organization in operation in France and felt that it could also work in the UK. Robert had become involved and, to cut a long story short, he asked me to chair a local committee to raise further funds. Thanks to the efforts of many people, well over £1 million was eventually raised, which enabled the community to become the self-sufficient unit it is today.

One of the important features of Emmaus is that it enables homeless people to regain their dignity as human beings through engaging in meaningful activity. Work is provided at each Emmaus site: recycling, renovating donated goods for sale in the Emmaus warehouse and other activities. Eventually a community will become self-supporting and then assist other groups to get started across the country. Today Cambridge has a turnover of approaching £1 million a year and has enabled many formerly homeless and despairing people to return to a greater fullness of life. There are now over 20 communities in the British Isles and many more in the process of development. Because of my experience of deprivation, Robert felt that I would have an understanding of the plight of the homeless and he invited me to succeed him as president of Emmaus UK.

When some people think of centres for the homeless they conjure up a picture of a doss-house or similar place. Emmaus is a million miles away from such a concept. Each community is there to enable people to help themselves by helping others and serving the wider community in which they are set. Night shelters and other such places are necessary to give respite, but for rehabilitation a different type of organization is needed, which Emmaus provides.

A new Emmaus community is never started until there are a substantial number of local people who understand the concept and are willing to commit themselves to raising funds to get the project under way, as well as doing all the necessary public relations work. It is a hard job, but if Emmaus is to be of real service to both the homeless and the wider community then it must be rooted in the locality.

One should never stereotype the homeless. They come from all walks of life. On a visit to a centre which provided respite for the homeless (not an Emmaus community), I wrote the following poem.

## HOMELESS

Words elude me.
I search for words
That will capture
The depth of my feeling.
That will hold within their shape
The pictures in my mind
And preserve them
Until the page fades
And dies,
As I shall die.

I see faces,
Many faces.
Unshaven,
Scarred.
Eyes.
Eyes that once sparkled with the innocence
    of childhood;
Eyes that once held promise;
Eyes now dulled
By the bitterness of life.

The room is full of faces.
They look at me
Quizzically,
Welcoming;
Each face holds a story
Of a life
That meanders aimlessly
Along grimy streets
Seeking scraps of meaning
Amongst the dereliction
Of the city.

I sit on a rough bench
With my ragged companions.
Some smile,
The wistful smile
Of souls
Condemned ever to wander,
Lost in the wilderness of mortal time,
Waiting for that day,
That hour,
When the flickering light
Will be no more.

My neighbour
Meticulously packs scraps of food
Into a plastic package.
Her head remains bowed.
The beauty of her face,
Enhanced by sadness,
Carries within it a lifetime of suffering.
A voice from across the table addresses me:
'She's blind you know.'

The other morning when we went outside, the meadow below the house was full of sheep but Dudley and Buster were nowhere to be seen. The next day I wrote to the owner of the property to let her know that all was well and in my email I mentioned the fact that the cattle had disappeared. She wrote back to say that there was nothing sinister. It seems that in the hot weather the farmer moves the cattle to a place where there is some shade. However, we miss them staring at us when we eat our meals on the outside veranda.

Last night there was a perfectly cloudless sky and being so far away from artificial lighting the heavens were clearly visible. The Southern Cross was unmistakable. Increasingly in many parts of the UK, because of light pollution, it is becoming harder and harder to view the night sky and it is so out here in the main cities. But this country place is ideal and that explains why there is a telescope in my bedroom which I have yet to use!

On a shopping expedition to Waipawa yesterday we called in at the Clock Shop to collect the new wristwatch strap I had previously ordered. Jim was busy at his workbench and was pleased as the day had started well with the sale of a large cuckoo clock to a passer-by. He and his wife Anne have invited the three of us to go round to their home this Saturday evening for a barbecue. Their invitation is typical of the friendliness of so many people in New Zealand. The small size of the population means that there is a slower pace of life here, making it an ideal country in which to relax.

This visit to New Zealand is partly a working visit and partly a holiday. Increasingly my wife dislikes long-distance air travel, and I can hardly blame her for that, so I have travelled to be with friends in New Zealand for the month. An elderly dog in London and three grandchildren living near to our home occupy much of her time. We are truly fortunate also to have a home in Suffolk where I keep my books and papers and attempt to do some writing. I spend quite a lot of time there alone as, ever since my days spent in solitary confinement, solitude appeals to me more and more. It's not that I don't want the company of others – I do and enjoy it much of the time. But the years in Beirut enabled me to enter into solitude and discover the benefits of so doing. It took a long time. When I was younger I was frequently told that I ought to make time to be alone for a while. When I did just that I found that I could not enjoy it as my mind was too active and I had not been able to separate myself sufficiently from my normal day-to-day activities. My captors, unknown to themselves, gave me many gifts, one of which is the ability now to be rejuvenated in solitude.

I wrote the following poem following a visit of children, grandchildren and others to Suffolk. I think it may describe what many grandparents feel. On the one hand they are delighted to welcome everyone. On the other it can be stressful. I hesitate to include this poem as when it is read by my family I really hope they will not stop visiting! One day, when they are older, they may understand more fully what I am attempting to say.

## EASTER HOLIDAYS

A holiday:
My silence is invaded
By laughing, excited children,
Glad to be released from the city,
Glad to be free in the countryside.

Our old dog,
Stiff with age,
Ambles into familiar territory
And finds her place
Under the kitchen bench.
Her two lively companions
Chase into the garden,
Happy to return to old haunts.

The family enter
And litter the room with cases,
Food,
Clothes,
Homework;
In a trice
A quiet haven
Is transformed
Into an emporium.

Now,
Expected, but without warning,
The tsunami enters
The vaulted kitchen,
Bags pile on empty surfaces,
Fridge doors open and close,
A kettle boils

And mugs,
Long unused,
Line up for regular duty.

I look at my children,
Always my children,
Even though the years
Have swallowed their youth.
My daughter glances across the room.
In a fleeting instance
I see my mother in her face,
Caught for a moment,
Then gone.
Sophie,
A grandchild,
Carries the eyes
Of her grandmother.

Here, assembled in this one room
Generations,
Living and departed,
Gather to drink tea;
In the brief time
They share space on earth.
In these short days together
We will laugh,
Eat and drink,
Delight in new discoveries.
I love them,
Love them all.
But ambiguity reigns.
My space is invaded,
Silence is absent,
Except in the dark reaches of the night.

I am divided
Through and through,
Wanting to be one with all,
Yet holding to my own, fragile, identity.

I continue to seek
The tranquillity
And wisdom
Due to my years.
The fractures in my soul
Run deep,
Protected by walls of silence.

Soon the holiday
Will be spent,
Soon the tide will recede,
Soon silence will descend,
Soon I shall be alone
With a fragile peace,
Soon this day will be but a memory,
Soon, mortal life will be spent.
God grant that I may live fully
Whilst I yet have earthly time.

The above poem was written over a long weekend at Easter, on the Saturday before Easter Sunday when I was left alone in the house while the family went on an outing to the sea.

It is difficult to pinpoint the age of our house in the country with any degree of accuracy, but it is believed that there has been a dwelling place on this site since the thirteenth century. The main living room has magnificent carved oak beams which have been identified as having been brought from the abbey at Bury St Edmunds when it was destroyed in Cromwellian times.

Situated on the village green, it was thought to have been a fairly large house belonging to the lord of the manor, and over 100 years ago was divided into two separate dwellings. A few years ago the house next door, formerly part of the one house, was rented by a couple with two small children. He was in the wine trade and she was a barrister. One day Nicola told me a very strange story indeed and to this day I can't make it out.

One evening she was bathing the two small children in the large bathtub upstairs when the telephone rang. As there was only a little water in the bath she stepped into the bedroom to answer it and returned to the bathroom within a minute or so. To her great surprise the two children, both too young to get out of the bath unaided, were standing on the bathmat. 'Goodness!' she cried, 'how did you get out?'

To her puzzlement the small boy replied that the old man had helped them out. 'Oh,' she said, 'and what was his name?' 'Kelly' was the reply she thought she heard.

When she told me this story I was amazed. 'Many years ago,' I said, 'my house was occupied by one named Kerry. Phil Kerry.' This was news to Nicola, who had no idea whatsoever of the previous occupants. Of course this whole episode might well have a perfectly rational explanation but I still find it a strange story.

Members of my family have been conscious of a friendly presence in the house and one of my daughters is convinced that she woke up one night when she felt someone sit on the end of her bed. Whoever, whatever, there is indeed a warm and good feeling about the house, and if it is haunted then I am perfectly prepared to share space with the unseen inhabitants.

During Good Friday, when all was quiet, I wrote the following lines.

## GHOSTLY FRIENDS

At last
I am alone.
Earlier, children, dogs,
With all other occupants of this house,
Tumbled joyfully into a car,
Picnic bound.
At last
I am alone.

The house breathes the silence of the ages.
Here in this very place
Families have lived,
And died,
Across a multitude
Of generations.
Some remain, their ghostly presence
Welcoming those who enter here.

Here under the oaken beams,
Lovingly carved
By skilful hands,
I sit
Alone with the company
Of those who departed mortal life
And now wait, silently,
Still holding to their former home.

Today,
A day of quiet,
When Christ lay silent in the tomb,
When women wept
And brave men despaired,

Today
I also wait.

The home
That sheltered so many
Is now my home;
A place of waiting,
Waiting for the resurrection
When all will be made new.
A false hope?
An empty promise?
Resurrection takes place within.
Here in the depth of soul
One may be renewed.
The life-giving spirit knows no bounds,
Is not confined to festivals.
The life-giving spirit
Moves where it will,
Transforming,
Healing.
Here in the silence
Of this ancient home,
I am at peace.
I wait with the ghosts of yesteryear,
I wait with hope in my heart.

The final poem in this trilogy reminds me that one ought not to wish life away. We will all have inner contradictions, but one ought to be grateful for the precious days which, as I say, are rapidly receding into memory.

## REMEMBER

Today a flurry of activity
As departure is prepared.
The washing machine toils incessantly,
Together with an overloaded dishwasher.
I stroll into the morning sunshine
Bemused by constant activity.
A final splendid breakfast is prepared:
Bacon, eggs, mushrooms, black pudding
And toast made on the Aga.
No other toast tastes like it!
We sit outside,
Around the long garden table,
As I delight in the company of my
    grandchildren:
Ella, tall, beautiful and full of life,
Sophie, quiet and reflective,
Sam, absent from the table,
Now perched at the top of a tree,
To the consternation of his anxious mother.

Will they remember these days?
Days when they caught small fish
In the stream behind the house
And Sophie named each one
After a member of the Royal Family.
Days when they collected moss and small
    flowers
To make a miniature garden for the table.
Days when they hunted high and low for
    eggs,
Carefully hidden in the garden.

Days when life with all its joys and perils
Lay before them.

The last bags are removed to the car;
The dogs settle in their special place,
Ready to sleep for the whole journey;
Farewells are said
And within a moment the house is silent.
I sit alone for a space.
Why in such precious moments of life,
Why do I feel overwhelmed?
Swamped by activity,
Exhausted by numbers.
I delight to see my family
And am relieved when peace returns.
Contradictions reign in my mind:
The need for others.
The need for solitude.

Remember these days my friend,
Remember these precious days.
Live life gently,
Savour the magic of the moment.
You are one of many faces
On a canvas larger than you know.
Remember these precious days,
They are receding into distant memory,
Remember . . .

Over 25 years ago I was invited to become a co-founder of an organization eventually called Y Care. Two young men, John Naylor and David Bedford, both then working for the Young Men's Christian Association (YMCA) came to see me at Lambeth Palace. They told me that the YMCA was one of the largest movements for young people in the world. There were over 70 million members worldwide, and in many countries the Y was a leader in social and welfare activities and widely respected for that. In the UK, they said, the public image was of an organization mainly engaged in providing gymnasia for young people, even though it was involved in many other social endeavours. They hoped to found an organization to utilize the global facilities of the worldwide YMCA and thus enable the really poor of this world to benefit. Thus Y Care was born.

Over the past quarter of a century thousands of youngsters who would normally never set foot in a YMCA have been aided through the work of Y Care.

Y Care does not send people out from the UK to run programmes of development. Rather, it provides funding and training support so that right from the start local people own their own projects and develop them. As there are functioning YMCAs in so many regions of the world the scope of Y Care's activities is wide. I have seen a village in Uganda transformed by the introduction of a protected spring, thus providing clean drinking water – a very simple programme indeed but one that has enabled countless people to enjoy better health. In South America I have seen young people break away from the gangs that had trapped them and begin to find meaningful ways of earning their own living. In Palestine I have sat with a therapist and listened as young people who have been imprisoned and tortured begin to come to terms with their experience.

I take no convincing that one of the best things we can do for teenagers is to help them to build good memories and begin to live and work creatively.

No matter how good the programme, and there are so many good and effective programmes around the world, one always has to struggle with the problems of human nature and the light and dark which exist within us all.

As human beings we are incomplete and programmes, no matter how good they are, will only go so far in enabling us to grow into our full stature as individuals. Harmonious relationships are not easily gained and certainly have to be worked for. I recollect reading a book many years ago entitled *The Wounded Healer*. The author pointed out that those who know their own deep inner wounds and have come to terms with them may well be in a stronger position to be supportive and understanding of others. The following poem speaks of a depth of understanding that can exist between two people which can be truly healing.

## A HIDDEN PLACE

Within my soul
Lies a hidden place,
A place of longing,
Longing to be free
From hurt
And that which would destroy.

Deep within
There is a wound,
Always protected
And guarded
From all
Excepting those
Who carry within
Their own
Pain.

Deep within,
In the mystery
Of unconscious life,
I know the secret you.
I know your inner longing,
Your inner pain.
For one brief moment,
Deep within.
We embrace,
And then we are gone.

The encounter
Reveals my incompleteness,
My fragile existence.
We embrace
And touch the hem
Of wholeness.

# 13 One to One

Earlier on I mentioned the involvement of Y Care in the Middle East. If I had to sum up in one word the main component that is lacking in the continuing conflict between Israel and the Palestinian Arabs it would be the word 'trust'. On the one hand the Israelis are terrified at the thought of losing territory and their control of water for the region. On the other the Palestinians are deeply angry at their loss of territory and the continued illegal occupation of what they regard as their land. There are admirable people, both Israeli and Palestinian, who are working together in an attempt to build trust and find a political solution, but a political solution will never be found until there can be a greater degree of trust between the two sides.

After I left captivity I met a remarkable man, David Altschuler. David lives in London, is Jewish and a humanitarian through and through. He came to the UK from South Africa 30 or so years ago and has established himself successfully in business, but his main love is working to make a difference to the lives of the disadvantaged throughout the world. He was a joint founder of the One to One Children's Fund and he and I have worked together across the years to promote some of the programmes the fund has started. Long before the South African government became realistic about the problem of HIV in southern Africa, David worked to help fund a programme designed to tackle this scourge. The programme has now developed right across the continent. In Kosovo he, together with his wife Jenny, set up a successful programme to aid children traumatized by war. In Israel and the Occupied Territories they support people from both sides of the divide who despite terrible odds work with the up and coming generation to aid the building of trust. As a patron of the Foundation, I have travelled with David to all three locations mentioned above and have given what support I can to his efforts.

My last visit to the region was just a few weeks before I came to New Zealand. I had gone with Y Care to support some of their projects. The gradual swallowing up of territory by the Israelis frequently brings me to the brink of despair. The following poem was written after I spent an afternoon in the ancient city of Hebron.

Hebron Market

## HEBRON

I stood in the old market
In Hebron.
A riot of colour
Blazed against the ancient stones.
Ladies' scarves,
Materials of every hue.
A cascade of plump oranges
Tumbled across a rough wooden stall.
An old man
Mixed perfumes,
Conjured from the very blooms
That garlanded a doorway.
I strolled on
Along the rough stone pathway
Trodden by generations
Of those for whom
This was home.

Now,
Some paces
Along the same pathway,
The colours have gone.
Shops stand shuttered
And empty.
A camera,
Fixed to a high post,
Stares down at me.
Razor wire,
As sharp as a thousand knives,
Blocks a street.
Onwards,

Beyond the electric eye,
Beyond the wire,
Soldiers linger in the shadows.
Suddenly
The air is torn
By a scream.
'Filthy Arabs. Go away.'
A demented settler
Raves from the protection
Of fortified apartments,
Pushing their way into the ancient
Heart of the city,
Seeking to possess
And control.

'Once,'
Says my guide,
'We had free passageway.
Today we are prisoners
in our own land.'

This is the Holy Land.
The Promised Land.
The Land of Milk and Honey.
Forgive me if I weep.

# 14 Belief

Good news! Dudley and Buster have returned!
Yesterday, when we came back from a quick visit
to the small town of Otane, there they were grazing
contentedly in the pasture by the house. We called out
their names and they raised their heads and bellowed
as though to acknowledge our greetings. Today it is
much cooler, which may account for their return.
There is a cold wind blowing from the Antarctic in the
south and snow is reported on the mountain tops near
to Christchurch. Given that it is midsummer here, that
might be considered to be unusual, although the locals,
in company with people the world over, say that the
seasons have gone haywire.

Otane is a small neat town which extends along one
main street. There is one general store, a post office
and a rather fine town hall. Leaving the town to join
State Highway 2, one crosses the railway line where,
when we arrived, a train carrying a massive load of
logs was en route, we assumed, to the port of Napier
and then onwards by ship to China.

In the 1980s I had the responsibility of arranging a
visit to New Zealand for the Archbishop of Canterbury
when the late Paul Reeves was Anglican Archbishop in
the country. Later, he resigned his position (but did not
resign from Holy Orders) to become Governor General,
a role in which he was immensely popular. He had
Maori blood in his veins and played a significant role
in promoting better relations between the different
ethnic groups in the country. Religion is often, and
sometimes justly, accused of being a major cause of

conflict in the world but it ought not to be forgotten that it has also played a significant role in peacemaking and peacekeeping.

Long before militant Islam raised its head and changed the dynamics of world politics, a colleague of mine at Lambeth Palace was insistent that Western governments did not take religion seriously enough. Subsequent events proved him correct. In the last two decades religion has been prominent and in many instances has been blamed for causing and perpetuating conflicts around the world. To put the total responsibility on religion is, in my opinion, incorrect. In making an analysis it can be seen as a part of a broader complex of factors which include social, cultural, ethnic and economic elements as well as the religious element.

In recent years certain religious groupings have dominated the world scene, from the extreme orthodox Jews in Israel to the fundamentalist Christians in the United States of America, to say nothing of the extremist elements in Islam. Anglicans have traditionally been seen to occupy 'middle ground' within the Christian tradition, but even they have been driven apart and in some cases to extremes by differences emanating from the cultures in which they are set. Nigerian culture is literally miles apart from the culture of southern California and the Anglican Church in both places is inevitably affected by the cultural norms operative in their own area. The Roman Catholic Church is able to hold together, albeit somewhat tenuously, by virtue of the fact that it has a strong central authority manifested in the Papacy, whereas Anglicans look to Canterbury and the Archbishop, who is recognized as *primus inter pares*, first among equals, with the other archbishops of the Communion. Canterbury can no more dictate orders to his fellow archbishops than the Pope can tell the Quakers of Bury St Edmunds how to conduct their affairs!

I was brought up within the Anglican tradition and have worked from a church base for much of my life. Although it was often suggested that I ought to become ordained I never had such a vocation and now, looking back, I realize that I was right not to go in that direction. So many people think that I am a clergyman due to the fact that I was a member of the Archbishop's staff, and I constantly have to correct that assumption. I remain grateful to Anglicanism for giving me so much, but in recent years have joined the Society of Friends (otherwise known as the Quakers) as a full member. Although it is not widely known, one may retain membership of the Anglican Church as well as being a member of the Friends. Perhaps I ought to be called a 'Quanglican'!

It was in captivity that I appreciated more fully the value of silence, and on my release I became increasingly restless with modern Anglican services of worship. There seemed to be so little opportunity for reflection, and corporate silence was virtually totally absent. For many years I had admired the Quakers for their ethical position and for their openness in respect of many doctrinal issues.

I wrote a poem with which I am not entirely satisfied but it at least contains some of the issues I was trying to grapple with.

### TRUTH?

Where lies truth?
Where lies the answer
To questions that trouble
A mind anxious for truth?

Some say the Church
Is where it may be found.
An 'ex cathedra' statement,

A rule,
An examined life.
The Church may point to truth,
Embody it?

Some say the Bible
Is the Word of God.
His Word is truth.
Should I then stone my neighbour?
Obey archaic demands?
Discernment must take place
By frail humans
Who search for truth.
The Bible is the truth?

Some say
The Spirit will guide
Into all truth.
Where and whom is Spirit?
Does Spirit speak equally
To the sane
And to those
Disturbed of mind?

In truth
We say we love.
What do we know
Of the inner workings of mind
Where,
In an instant,
Truth may vanish
Like a spectre in the night?

The American lawyer and civil rights campaigner Clarence Darrow is quoted as saying, 'I don't believe in God because I don't believe in Mother Goose.' Well, I once knew of an Anglican clergyman named Father Goose and you can guess what name we attributed to his wife! More seriously, there is a great deal of discussion these days about God and I confess to having sympathy with those who raise their voice in support of atheism. However, I do sometimes wonder why they have to be so vehement in their protestations, for it seems to me that atheism is simply the other side of absolute belief. Surely, the only true scientific position to take is that of the agnostic. I have never met Richard Dawkins who, quite rightly in my opinion, promotes scientific inquiry, but could it be that in his approach to religion he is asking the wrong sort of questions?

At the heart of our existence lies a deep mystery and to give meaning and coherence to life people everywhere find concepts and images that enable that mystery to be more fully comprehended. Of course there will be those who take religion absolutely literally just as there are those who understand the various stories as pointing to spiritual truths.

Christ himself was not really a 'religious' man: in fact he deeply upset the religious personages of his day. It has been my experience that when I have met individuals from different theistic traditions and learned something of their experience there has been a great deal of common agreement about matters spiritual. There is no doubt that 'religion' has been a contributor to many evils in the world, just as it has inspired much that is good and wholesome. The following lines, in the final verse of the next poem, might, I trust, capture something of the essence of what Christ himself taught and practised.

## THE KINGDOM*

There is a realm
Beyond time,
Immune to the rigours
Of inquiry
That formulate,
Measure
And categorize.

Familiar tools
Fail to illuminate
The highways
Of this kingdom.
A kingdom
Without height,
Breadth,
Depth.
A kingdom
Infinite.
Not of this world,
But embedded
In the depths
of soul.

How can we know
Such a mystery?
How can we touch
The intangible?
How can we prove
That which cannot be captured
In scientific tables?

---

* Dedicated to Kathy Ertel.

Be still.
Listen to the inner voice.
Learn to love.
Let compassion
Guide your actions.
Walk calmly
Through the mists
Of unknowing.
The kingdom is yours.

Today there was a message from someone who had read one of my books, *Taken on Trust*. This book was written in my head during the years of captivity when I was denied pen or paper and much later written down when I was elected as Fellow Commoner of Trinity Hall, Cambridge. In that book I recount something of the experience of those years. 'What I don't understand,' said the questioner, 'is why you did not experience more anger towards your captives and why you are not angry today.'

Initially I was angry. I was angry with my captors for breaking their word when they had given me a promise of safe conduct. It was when I grew to understand the reasons for their behaviour that my anger dissipated. Although I did not agree with their actions I could understand their behaviour, misguided as it was. I would not say in any way that I am a soft sentimentalist but over the years I have met hundreds of people, both men and women, languishing in the prisons of our land. When one gets to know them and their background then frequently one has a better understanding as to why they were led into crime. I know full well that there are lots of people who have had a difficult childhood with no real family life, and no adequate support when growing up, and have managed to make something of their life. But circumstances vary. As for my captors, many of them were recruited into the ranks of a terrorist organization when they were at an impressionable age. Once inside then there was no retreat. I have frequently quoted the story of one young guard who cheated the terrorist organization when given money to buy food for captives and tried the old trick of pocketing half for himself. When his duplicity was uncovered he was taken and shot! If he cheated the organization on small matters, what would he do if he was offered a large bribe to betray the organization, reasoned his superiors.

Also, I have seen so many people who have suffered a terrible personal tragedy when a child of theirs has been murdered or they themselves have been victim of a violent attack. They have been understandably angry and have allowed that anger to fester until their own life has been almost totally destroyed. Anger should not be allowed to turn to bitterness, for bitterness is like a cancer that enters the soul. It does more harm to those who hold it than it does to those against whom it is held.

I don't want to lose the capacity to be angry, but I hope that I shall be able to deal with my anger in such a way that it can be turned and used for creative ends.

These few lines sum up something of what I believe.

### ANGER

Anger rages
Like a consuming fire,
Destroying all
That would impede
Its relentless pathway.

Do not extinguish
The flames totally.
Calm them.
And warm yourself
By the gentle glow
Of the embers.

During the course of the many interviews that I have given in the past years I am frequently asked who are my heroes. I have difficulty in answering this question as I do not idolize other human beings, but of course I do deeply respect and admire many for their various abilities. One such person whom I respect for his academic capacity, and for his remarkable bravery, is the late Tony Judt. Judt was an historian of undoubted ability, a social critic and a very brave man. I first came across his writings in the *New York Review of Books* when it published a series of essays he had written during the closing stages of his life. He had been diagnosed with a form of motor neurone disease and gradually the muscles in his body had begun to fail until he was totally paralysed. His final book, *Thinking in the Twentieth Century*, was dictated to his long-standing friend the historian Timothy Snyder, and I am currently reading it.

One cannot read about Tony Judt without reflecting on suffering and how it is no respecter of persons. It strikes where it will with an impersonal savagery that can cripple and destroy. Judt is a very recent example of how the deepest suffering can be faced and turned to a creative end. He was not totally destroyed by it but, despite it, enabled others to benefit from his critical and compassionate insight through his writings.

The following few lines are my way of saying that, no matter how we try, there is no satisfactory answer to the problem of suffering. All we can do, as human beings, is to be compassionate to others and to ourselves and gladly offer the hand of compassion to those who need it.

## YOU ASK ME WHY?

You ask me why
The innocent suffer,
A child dies at birth,
A father remains
As sole provider,
A victim cries
When vandals
Destroy his home?
You ask me why
And I am silent.

Suffering stalks the land
Striking whom it will
With inhuman vengeance
And bloody force.

You ask me why?
And I am silent.
I take your hand in mind
As together
We tread the pathway of sorrow.
No words suffice
At this time of anguish.

Just a couple of weeks left and we will leave this house for the next stage of this winter journey spent in warmer weather. I don't want to leave as the peace and serenity of this location speak directly to my soul and I feel totally at home here. Each morning following breakfast I sit down to write and most days my companions leave to explore the surrounding area or to do some essential shopping. We jointly prepare a meal in the evening and then Jenny will proofread, organize and print what I have written and add it to the growing manuscript. I am never satisfied with my writing and need the reassurance of others. Jenny urges me to continue and I do so in the hope that some of the things I have written will speak to those who read them.

When we finally say goodbye to this place we shall travel to Auckland and join a ship on which I shall be giving several lectures between New Zealand and Singapore. Last year I travelled on board a ship where the cruise was especially designed for older passengers. It's really encouraging to see just how many people, some well into their nineties, get out and about. It was through meeting people on board who had spent a lifetime together that I wrote the following lines.

## TILL DEATH DO US PART

A grey haired man,
Clad in voluminous khaki shorts
Which in an instant betray his generation,
Passes by.

His face?
Lined,
Not only with the passing of years
But with a sorrow
Borne with quiet dignity.
Compassionate,
Undemonstrative.

He clasps the hand of his wife
Who trails behind.
Her body
Contorted and twisted,
Bent double.
Her only vision being of the ground
Over which she stumbles.
'In sickness and health
Till death do us part'.
The words strike home.

Was she once pretty?
Did she dance?
Play the piano?
Captivate with her passion for life?

She shuffles along the deck,
Along the corridor of life
Into a future without respite
For a broken body.
In sickness and health,
So help me God.

Although here in the countryside we are miles away from major centres of population and I never switch on the TV and rarely listen to the radio, I do read a downloaded British newspaper each day. The downloading is painfully slow and each evening we wait impatiently as we like to complete the crossword as we prepare the evening meal. So far our best time is 13 minutes and our worst is about 80.

The newspaper details many stories of family horrors. Children murdered because they brought dishonour on their religious parents by wearing short skirts and straying from their strict code of behaviour; a suicide supposedly because a marriage was facing difficulties; lonely individuals seeking an ideal partner. One could go on and on. Recently, in discussing marriage relationships with a friend, I came out with the following words and she quickly scribbled them down in shorthand and gave them to me some weeks later.

## KNOWING – NOT KNOWING

I knew you
But I never knew you.
I saw you
But I never saw you.

We walked together
Through life
With faltering steps.
Half hoping,
Half dreaming
That life would bind us deeply together.

In the eyes of God we were one.
As we looked into each other's eyes,
The distance was immeasurable.

We are incomplete within ourselves and sometimes impossible demands are made by one partner on the other to fill that lack. Perhaps the most satisfactory relationship between two people is where the relationship enables each to be more complete, rather than one party being robbed of identity, or dominated by the other.

The Hawke's Bay area where we are staying is famous for good wines. I gave up all alcohol some years ago in order to lose weight and have never gone back, but I still appreciate the bouquet of a good wine! Last evening we drove across to have dinner with Chris Pask, who came to New Zealand over 30 years ago and started what is now one of the leading wineries in the country. The Pask family farm is in the village where we have a home in Suffolk and at one time, many years ago, Chris's uncle, and before that his grandfather, lived in the house that we now occupy in the village. Chris confirmed that the beautiful carved beams in the living room of my house came from the great abbey at Bury St Edmunds which was destroyed by the citizens of that town in the seventeenth century.

Chris and Alyson had invited some of their friends to dinner, two of whom had lived in Uganda where I had lived when I was a young man. We knew many people in common and it was fun to recount days long past.

Memories . . . last evening brought back African years about which I have written more extensively in an earlier book. To celebrate my seventieth birthday I took my wife, children and grandchildren back to Uganda to see the place where our son was born and our three daughters started school. We returned to look at our former home in Kampala. When we lived there it had a lovely garden, which was now no more. Kampala had been transformed from an attractive capital city to a dreadful urban sprawl. We travelled along by the River Nile to Murchison Falls set in the National Park, but

17 Memories

even this part of Uganda is now threatened as oil has been discovered and this does not bode well for this region. Of course, it will bring economic wealth and I wonder if I am being unduly cynical if I have my doubts as to whether or not this wealth will be properly used.

Nigeria, in West Africa, ought to be one of the most developed countries in the whole of the African continent given the vast sums of money that have been generated by oil exploitation. Instead there is poverty on a grand scale and many areas of the country have been polluted and spoiled. Zimbabwe, once the bread basket of Africa, is an economic disaster. One could go on and I do not want be over-pessimistic. I love many parts of that great continent, but there is no doubt whatsoever that so many African countries have been ill served by their political leaders who have grown rich on the backs of the majority of the population, who have remained in grinding poverty.

The following poem contains some of the images that are in my mind when I think of Africa, and Uganda in particular.

## LAKE VICTORIA

An early morning mist,
Spreading like tattered cotton sheets
Across Lake Victoria.
The silence at dawn
When slowly
The horizon emerges
From slumber
And a thousand colours
Dispel
The blackness of night.
The pungent odour of damp earth.
Earth that gave life.
Earth to which we shall return.

A gecko,
Motionless on a window pane,
Waiting to strike
As Africa waits
To smite the unwary.
Thin wisps of smoke
Spiral upwards
Into the once black sky.
A baby cries.
A skeleton of a dog,
Eyes ablaze,
Scavenges,
As all Africa scavenges,
For life.
A woman,
Busuuti clad,
Sings as she walks.
An old man,
White kanzu,
Black coat,
Leans heavily on a gnarled stick.

Now the tattered mist
Is no more.
Now the colours have faded.
Now the red dust swirls through the air
As the sun pursues
Its merciless trek
Across the heavens.
A new day
Is born
As the dog scavenges
And the old man
Leans on his gnarled stick.

Lake Victoria

For those not familiar with East Africa, a busuuti is a traditional
dress worn by many African women, introduced into that country,
I believe, by the Victorians. A kanzu is a long white robe principally
worn by Muganda men.

Fewer than two weeks left before we depart from this
stage of our winter journey and travel to Auckland.
Near to where we are staying, a bridge about a quarter
of a mile in length crosses the Tukituki. It is a single-
lane bridge and requires frequent repair as the hills on
the far bank are gradually pushing at it, causing it to
need regular attention. This morning I spent a little
time reading about the history of this region of Hawke's
Bay. Almost all the early settlers came here from
England or Scotland in the mid-nineteenth century
and eventually established some very prosperous farms.
Just by the bridge is the Patangata Tavern, which at one
time was quite an elegant building surrounded by a
cooling veranda. Alas, that building caught fire and has
been replaced by a hideous structure which does no
justice whatsoever to the surrounding natural beauty.
However, in all fairness, I must say the food was good
as one evening we went there for a change and enjoyed
really well-cooked fish and chips!

**TUKITUKI**

The Tukituki
Sparkles
In the noonday sun,
Meandering gently
Through pastures green,
And luscious.
Brown trout
Laze in cooling waters.

Sheep,
Too numerous to be
counted,

Graze silently
On the slopes
Surrounding the house.
Two longhorn cattle
Lift their heads
As though to greet us
In our new home.

Overnight
A carpet of yellow flowers
Has sprung
From fertile soil.
The gentle wind
Whispers and dances,
Urging all
Whom it touches
To join
And skip through the valley.

Night falls
And all is silent.
The heavens sparkle
With a million diamonds.

The Tukituki,
Never sleeping,
Flows through the darkness
To the great sea.
The wind rests.
In the silence of night
We rest,
At one
With creation,
On our journey
To the great sea of unknowing.

Tukituki

The Tukituki river valley

# 19 Delusion

Mental illness is a growing problem within our society and each week brings me letters from people who appear to be deeply troubled of mind. I understand that one in four of the population will suffer from some type of mental instability at one time or another. That is an alarming number, particularly as mental health care is a Cinderella of the National Health Service.

I have spent time in the last years meeting and talking with staff and patients at Rampton, a hospital for the criminally insane. There are three such institutions in England: Rampton, Broadmoor and Ashworth. All three places are kept totally secure, but they are not prisons and do not come under the purview of the Prison Service, although all the patients have committed criminal acts. I have the greatest respect for the staff who work in these hospitals, and as a country we can be justly proud that we do give such a high standard of care to some of the most dangerous members of society.

The following lines speak of a visit to my office in Lambeth made over 40 years ago, but still fresh in my mind.

## NUMBERS

He entered my office.
Tall,
Debonair,
A well-cut suit
And polished brown shoes
Projected assurance.

'I have a solution for you!'
The words flew quickly
From his anxious lips.
No time for
Pleasantries.
No pause to order coffee.
He fumbled
In an inner pocket.

A scribbled note
Thrust hastily
Across my desk.
'Read it,'
He commanded.
His eyes fastened intently
On the jottings
As though they might fly from the room
And escape the clutch of their creator.

'Read it. Quickly.
Time is precious.'
I scanned the incomprehensible
Numbers.
'What does it mean?'
A naive question.

Now assurance had flown
The tie was loosened
And acute distress
Crossed the contours
Of his face.

'Look. Can't you see?
Ireland – the solution!
3
5
894
28.'

Later,
He left his wife
And disappeared
From the face of the earth.
Did numbers
Ever reconcile
His inner contradictions?
Was he ever reconciled within?

3
5
894
28
He walked away
Leaving me with numbers,
And many questions.

Only a few days left of our stay. Tomorrow the owners of the property will come over and have dinner with us and on Saturday morning we will leave by car for Auckland and join the ship. It is with considerable reluctance that I prepare to say farewell to this place. To be fortunate enough to have a whole month away and have time to reflect on past events is a real luxury. My secretary, Sarah, who is back in the UK, emailed me last night to say that the BBC had been in touch as today, 20 January, was the very date on which I started my long sojourn in captivity. They wanted to do a live interview and so tonight I will take their call. I am hopeless when it comes to remembering dates and had no idea at all that today was a marking point in my life.

I have often said that whenever a person is taken hostage the family and friends of the individual are taken captive also. This is a deeply frightening and difficult experience for them. They may or may not get assistance from the employer of the hostage, but they certainly will get offers of help from the Foreign and Commonwealth Office and the Police Family Support Unit. However, as so many families can testify, there is no substitute for being able to be in touch with and receive support from others who have passed through a similar experience.

Many people who were in distress contacted me personally across the years since my release and I did what I could to assist them. However, as the demands increased I felt that I ought to set up an organization which would be able to put such help on a sound basis, and thus Hostage UK was born. Carlo Laurenzi, who had previously worked with Prisoners Abroad, joined me and together we put together a small charity. We deliberately keep 'lean and light' as we have no central office. Our truly excellent part-time co-ordinator, Rachel Briggs, works from home and we have been fortunate in getting together a first-rate group of trustees with a wide range of experience.

The following lines are an attempt to illustrate part of the experience of someone who has lost a family member through hostage-taking. For some the agony continues for years.

### THE NIGHT HOURS

It is the night hours.
The time when all is still,
Bar the creaks,
As the old house
Settles before dawn.

In the far distance
A police siren
Wailing through the night air,
Prompting
A thousand thoughts.
Where is he?
Does he suffer?
Do they hurt him?
Will we ever meet again?

Once again
Silence,
Deep silence.
Sleep,
Ever evasive,
Hides its face.

On one occasion I was asked to visit the mother of someone who had been brutally murdered in Iraq. Naturally, the elderly lady was deeply upset and even further disturbed when she learned her son had been decapitated. When I arrived at her home, somewhere in the UK, she was in bed, having recently received this distressing news. We spoke together for quite some time and just before I left she looked directly at me and said, 'You know, to lose a son in this way is terrible, just terrible. However, my suffering is no different from that of an Iraqi mother who has lost her child through war or terrorism.' I shall always remember the compassion, the deeply felt empathy, this lady showed at a time of acute suffering for herself and her family.

Quite a long time afterwards I wrote the following few lines.

### PAIN

The pain
Sears my soul,
Penetrates to the very depth
Of my being.

At night,
Alone,
I weep
The tears
Of anguish,
Of loss,
Of despair.

Take heart.
Through pain
You have entered
A new realm.
You have joined

The community of compassion.
Your sorrow will be turned
To joy,
Your tears
Will become laughter,
Your wound will remain,
But now through suffering,
You have a new depth of soul.

It was with real sadness that we left the house to travel some six or so hours to Auckland. On the evening of our final night the owners of the property came round and cooked us all a most splendid meal. Needless to say, delicious New Zealand lamb was on the menu! We left early the following morning, travelling for some miles by the Tukituki and through rolling countryside full of sheep and cattle. We drove for at least three hours before we met significant traffic, and even then it was nothing compared to the traffic at home in the UK. I said it was with sadness that I left the New Zealand countryside, for after spending a lifetime travelling throughout the world it was here that I felt at home and felt sure that I would return.

One of the great features of Auckland is that ships dock right in the town and so one can leave the ship and, within a few moments, walk into the city. I have sailed in and out of this harbour many times and it never fails to interest me.

Of course, many passengers leave their ships here after having been on board for several weeks and this is the place where they say goodbye to friends made during the course of the voyage. Some will keep in touch across the years – others they will never see again.

After watching people come and go I wrote the following.

## FRIENDS

The days come and go,
But some days remain in the mind for ever.
A busy day
Packing,
A hurried breakfast,
A hug, a kiss, a thousand times:
'Lovely journey',
'See you in England',
'Don't forget to write.'
Newfound friends dressed in their
    travelling clothes.
Friends? Perhaps.
Perhaps one day we shall meet again,
But life will have gone by
And we will all be changed.
A final departure as ship gives way to shore.
Now I sit alone,
Deeply alone,
In a crowd of departing 'friends'.
Now I see you.
A friend?
I see you.
A face touched and mellowed by pain.
I see you.
Eyes,
Behind which tears linger.
I hold you and words have left me.
A friend?
The word is inadequate,
As all words are inadequate.
For a space we have been brought together,
Now we part,
Waiting to be separated by distance,
Longing to be united in spirit.

The journey from Auckland to Singapore passed through many of the ports in Australia and Indonesia that I had previously visited. A cruise is certainly a good means by which one may get a quick impression of the country the ship is visiting, but it can be nothing more than a quick impression.

Indonesia, for example, seen through the eyes of a tourist is very different from that seen from the perspective of an aid worker. Years ago, when I was a young man, I stayed in one of the poor areas of Jakarta during the monsoon season. I was fortunate to be staying in a house, but in the street outside there were families living beneath sheets of plastic and attempting to survive and bring up a family under such conditions. One very rainy night a mother gave birth in her primitive shelter. On board I cannot help but feel the tremendous gap that exists between the very poor of this world and the affluent. Many of us, in our respective ways, try to help through working with, or giving to, aid organizations, but at the end of the day charity alone is not the answer. There has to be a more radical and fundamental change in the global economy and I do not see that happening in the foreseeable future.

One of the Indonesian islands we visited, which depends exclusively on tourism, was the island of Komodo. This is one of over 17,500 islands that make up the Republic of Indonesia. There are just 2,000 people on Komodo and many have former convicts as their ancestors as they were exiled there many years ago.

The island is famous, not for its convicts but for the formidable Komodo dragons which roam freely across the territory. These strange animals, the heaviest lizards on earth, can reach roughly ten feet in length and weigh over 300 pounds. These carnivores are extremely dangerous and will eat humans given a chance! With two expert local

Komodo dragon

guides a small party of us from the ship set off to trek to the interior in search of these strange beasts. We were lucky. After half an hour or so we came to a clearing in the forest and there, facing us, were five dragons, dripping their deadly bacteria-ridden saliva and staring at us. Our guides urged us to stand perfectly still and not to alarm them in any way. All that stood between us tasty mortals and a dragon was a five-foot-nothing Indonesian with a forked stick! We were told that should they spring the guide would poke them in the eyes with this implement. Fortunately, after several minutes the dragons ambled off to be lost in the bush. We did as we were instructed and managed to get some photographs of this primitive species.

Several weeks have passed since I came back from New Zealand and immediately on my return I was thrown into activity, leaving me no time at all to write. Now, thanks to the kindness of friends, I am hidden away in Cornwall for several days and can complete this brief manuscript.

The last poem was an attempt to capture some of the mixed emotions that face those who have spent time together and then part, perhaps never to meet again. Like many of my poems it is intended to capture feelings which I think are common to many.

I value and respect the desire of my family for their privacy and that is why, with one small exception, they are not immediately obvious in this book. We have four children, all strong-minded and all, in their own way, travellers. As I write my son has just returned from the base camp at Everest and goodness knows where my daughters will travel to this year. They belong to a generation that is at home in any part of the world where they happen to find themselves.

Now, alone for several days in Cornwall, I pick up the threads of this book. I need a day or so to let my mind settle after the turmoil of dealing with a host of difficult problems. The following lines attempt to express something of what I feel as once more I commit pen to paper.

## NO GREAT THOUGHTS

I lie awake
As dawn breaks;
No great thoughts
Cross my mind.
No words flow
To capture
What I feel.

My feelings are scattered
Like chaff in the wind;
I see my children
In lands afar,
In a trice
I am home,
As the first stirrings of the day
Rumble through the house.

My mind moves
From scene to scene
With a speed
Unequalled by science.
I cross the bounds of time
To childhood,
To a world full of promise:
I cross the continents
To captivity,
To a world full of threat;
I move with lightning speed,
Not stopping to ponder.
Now I return
To my quiet room,

No great thoughts,
No easy flow of words.

The light of day enters
My lonely room,
Filled with those far away,
Brought into mind
To comfort and embrace.
No great thoughts
Today,
No flow of words,
Just a ramble
Through the scraps of memory,
Just a stirring of mind
As one enters a new day.

## 23  A gathering

The radio van, belonging to BBC Cornwall, has just left the house as I pick up my pen to write once more. Later in the week I shall be speaking at an evening designed to attract support for a new Emmaus community we are in the process of developing here in Cornwall, and my interview this morning was to publicize that event. It's an overcast and cold Sunday morning and I miss the warmth of a New Zealand summer even though I am staying in a lovely part of the country.

Last night I watched a TV programme in which my old friend John Sergeant travelled throughout the British Isles with various groups of foreign tourists. One of the places he visited was Llangollen, in North Wales, where each year an international music festival is held. This festival was started by local people after the Second World War and is designed to promote peace through the language of the arts, principally music. Musicians and others from all corners of the globe gather together in Llangollen each July and for one full week this little Welsh town is transformed.

One of the first groups to arrive for the inaugural festival, in 1947, came from Portugal. They made the journey across Europe in an ancient charabanc and caused great excitement as they drove down the main street of the town. Subsequently there have been countless emotional moments but perhaps one of the most memorable took place in 1949. In the July of that year a young man, Hywel Roberts, was asked to compere the International Mixed Choir competition. This was not an easy task for him as on the final day of the Second World War his brother had been killed in action in Germany. Standing in the wings, ready to perform, was the Lübeck Choir from West Germany. The audience waited anxiously, wondering how Hywel would cope with this situation. In the true spirit of the Eisteddfod he made an emotional appeal that the choir be greeted as 'our friends from West Germany'.

The following poem was written, at the request of the current musical director, Eilir Owen Griffiths, to be set to music to commemorate the seventieth year of the festival.

### THE ASHES OF WAR

The ashes of war
Litter the ground
Where men have fought
And died.

The wind blows cold
Across the fields.
The wind blows cold today.

The weapons of war
Are silent now
Where men have fought
And died.

The wind blows hard
Across the fields.
The wind blows hard today.

The burden of war
Has muted our song
Where men have fought
And died.

The wind blows harsh
Across the fields.
The wind blows harsh today.

We hear the echo
Of a song
Where men have fought
And died.

A gentle song,
A healing song,
A song that rises from the dust
And calms the troubled mind.

The wind has calmed
Across the fields
Where men have fought
And died.
A gentle voice
Proclaims a hope,
That from the ashes of despair
A harmony will rise.

In Cymru's fields
A healing wind
Breathes harmony and peace,
And from the ashes of despair
A thousand voices
Fill the air,
Blest is the world that sings.

The nations gather
From afar,
Their voices are as one.

The children laugh, and dance and sing,
Their voices through the valleys ring.
The ashes now,
Ablaze with light,
Blest is the world that sings,
Blest is the world that sings.

Some years ago the committee of the festival wrote to me inviting me to be president, and I replied that I was honoured to be asked but I was not Welsh. Back came the reply reminding me that this was an international festival and urging me to accept. Accept I did and the following lines give a little of the flavour of the week. The word *eisteddfod* is Welsh, of course, and simply means 'a gathering'.

The International Music Eisteddfod parade

## EISTEDDFOD

'Not Lann
But Thlann.'
My first instruction
In the language
Of the bards.
The language
Where music
Resounds through the valleys
Transforming
The grimy realities
Of a workaday world,
Warming those who are caught
In the melody of the ages.

The field is a symphony of colour,
An unrehearsed cacophony
Of nations,
Waiting with excitement,
When in song and dance,
They reveal the soul
Of their homeland.

Now
In the great pavilion
They march.
Drummers,
Dancers,
Singers,
National flags
Borne proudly aloft,
Ready to blend together
Through the language
In which they are all one.

The river flows onwards
Through the town.
Young boys dive
Into its cooling waters.
People throng the streets.
In the near distance
The gentle strains of music
Reach out into the world.

Be healed.
Be at peace.
Let the harmony of nations
Enter your soul.
Sing with joy,
Today, we are one.

Across the years Llangollen has attracted musicians who, as their
career developed, became household names. The young Pavarotti
travelled to Wales from Modena as a junior member of his father's
choir. Later, he returned as a soloist and now, following his death,
each year the Pavarotti Trophy is eagerly sought by aspiring young
musicians.

One memorable evening at Llangollen I first met the Welsh composer
Karl Jenkins when he was conducting his magnificent work *The
Armed Man*. This spectacular piece was accompanied by video clips
shown on two large screens on either side of the stage where the
evils of war were portrayed in graphic detail. Karl told me afterwards
that he was working on a new composition dealing with the theme
of peace. It was his intention to include the sayings of various
peacemakers: Gandhi, Martin Luther King, Nelson Mandela and
others. To my surprise he asked me if I would be able to contribute
something and with some degree of trepidation I agreed.

The weeks passed by and when I went to Cornwall for a few days, sitting at the very table I am now sitting at, I wrote the following lines which I sent off to Karl in Wales. With his usual skill and sensitivity he set them to music and they were beautifully sung by the soprano Lucy Crowe. The premiere of this work took place in New York at the Carnegie Hall, and on 20 May 2012 it was performed to a capacity house in the Royal Festival Hall, London. Immediately before the performance I hosted a reception for the One to One Children's Fund and launched a project designed to support Israeli and Palestinian children, many of whom have been traumatized by warfare. Although the situation in the Middle East is dire, I said that we must keep hope alive and continue to work for a peaceful resolution to the issues that have caused so much suffering across the years.

PEACE . . .

Peace is the fragile meeting
Of two souls in harmony.

Peace is an embrace
That protects and heals.

Peace is a reconciling
Of opposites.
Peace is rooted in love,
It lies in the heart,
Waiting to be nourished,
Blossom
And flourish,
Until it embraces the world.

May we know the harmony of peace,
May we sing the harmony of peace,
Until in the last of days,
We rest in peace.

Just before I came down to Cornwall for a few days
I visited my old friend the painter John Bellany RA.*
John was remarkable. Almost 30 years ago another
friend of mine, the eminent surgeon Roy Calne, gave
John a liver transplant with the result that John was
the second longest survivor of such radical surgery.
The other survivor was just a month or so ahead of
him. In our time both John and I had been elected as
Fellow Commoners at Trinity Hall, Cambridge, where
Roy, no mean artist himself, was also a Fellow.

It was at Trinity Hall that I put down on paper the
book which I had written in my head during the long
years of solitary confinement. To this day I remain ever
grateful to Cambridge, and Trinity Hall in particular,
for providing me with the opportunity to write and
return to life at a pace I could manage. When the
manuscript was completed I went to visit John at his
home and studio some few miles outside Cambridge
and as I read a couple of chapters aloud he painted
my portrait. Just before we parted on that occasion he
suggested that I ought now to try writing some poetry.
Almost 20 years later, having started on some of the
works recorded in this small volume, I remembered
what he had said. John was still painting vigorously.
His large studio was packed with canvasses and the
house was full of his distinctive works. Over tea
I read him something of what I have written and he
began another portrait, thus repeating the experience
of 20 years past.

---

* John Bellany RA died 28 August 2013.

In company with so many artists, John was a passionate man. By
that I mean he was sensitive and in touch with his feelings. I read
the following two poems to him.

## BY THE SHORE

I stood on the shore of sanity
Gazing into waters of abandon,
Stretching far into the distance.

The waters beckoned,
Come,
Swim, cast away your clothes of convention,
Position,
Family;
Come,
Swim.

Are there not calmer waters?
Waters where I may swim
Freely,
Waters where I shall not drown?

I turned and saw another sea.
The waters beckoned,
Come, swim.
These waters also
Lap the shores of sanity.
Come as you are.
No promises can be given
But come prepared;
These waters can heal,
But many have drowned
As they plunged unheeded
Into the deep.

These are the waters of love,
Of Eros, Agape, Philia;
These are the waters where Venus
Seizes the unprepared,
And in a moment of passion,
Drags them to certain death.

These waters lap the shores of sanity;
Calm,
Turbulent,
Dangerous,
As deep as you wish to go,
Come prepared,
Before you swim,
Consider,
Do not cast all away,
Be gentle,
Very gentle;
Feel the warmth of healing love
As you step into the deep.
Keep sight of shore,
Swim
And be healed.

## PASSION

My passions run high.
They rage and churn
Like a mighty river
Plunging headlong
O'er crags and boulders,
Rushing forward,
Onwards,
Sweeping all before
Leaving me breathless,
Taking me onwards
Through to a sea
As yet unexplored,
Deep,
Mysterious,
My passions run high.

My passions are gentle.
Gentle as a river
That calmly
Meanders through a glade,
Still and deep
And quiet.
Here in these gentle waters
I may rest awhile,
Conscious of the deep,
Resting in the calm.
My passions are gentle.

Join me my darling,
Cast aside your cares,
Step naked into the waters.
Feel the cool waters

Caress your breasts,
Filling you with life,
Commanding you to swim,
To swim through the shallows,
To enter the raging torrent,
To be seized by uncontrollable forces
That leave you breathless
And fulfilled.

Our passions run high.
Two rivers have met.
Now,
As one,
They plunge forward
To that great sea of unknowing,
That sea where once they enter
They shall be no more.
How far? You ask
How far before our passions die
And we are no more.
We cannot know my love.
We cannot tell.
We only know now.
The calm,
The torrent,
The flowing together,
Always together,
Until we are no more.

I began this small book by reflecting on death and that theme recurs in many of the poems I have included. Hardly a week has passed recently without a friend, or someone whom I have known well, having died. Recently a former sailing companion and good friend, Edwin Boorman, owner of the Kent Messenger Group, died. Edwin was truly a man of Kent and most generous to his friends and to many charitable causes, of which the Order of St John was one of his particular favourites.

He was a passionate sailor and his 42-footer, *The Messenger*, was his pride and joy. He knew every inch of that boat and seemingly could repair the most obscure engine fault or decide with impeccable skill whether or not to deploy the spinnaker. My wife Frances and I frequently sailed with him out of Gibraltar where, for a while, he moored the boat. On one memorable occasion we were sailing into harbour when we saw the massive form of the *Queen Elizabeth 2* approaching us. As I knew Ron Warwick, the then captain of the liner, we got on the radio and, working on the principle that 'steam gives way to sail', asked if the *QE2* would kindly move over. I will not repeat the reply we got, but all I will say is that we deserved it!

One January, a party of six of us, including Edwin and his wife, flew to Moscow at Orthodox Christmas to join the Trans-Siberian Express bound for Beijing. As both Edwin and I are reputed to snore we shared a compartment, while Frances and Edwin's wife Jeanine shared the compartment next door. As it was Orthodox Christmas, on Christmas Eve we attended a memorable

performance of *The Nutcracker* at the Bolshoi and the very next day
visited a supermarket where we bought enough basic provisions to
last us until we reached China. We had been told, quite correctly as it
turned out, that the restaurant car on the train was somewhat basic. It
was indeed and we used it only once, when we had a very greasy fried
egg and something that passed for bacon but resembled nothing that
I had previously come across. Although the washroom was primitive
we did enjoy the benefit of natural refrigeration. To move from one
car to another one had to pass through a connecting passage which
was exposed to the outside temperature. As that was frequently
40 degrees below we could hang our perishable provisions there in
plastic bags, where they froze solid.

The several days spent on the train passed very quickly indeed. We
had occasional stops at small railway stations where women on the
platform sold bread, hard-boiled eggs and roast chickens. The one
lengthy stop of 13 hours was on the border between Russia and China
where the bogies on the carriages were changed due to the fact that
the two countries run on different gauge rails. I have actually forgotten
the name of the town but it was utterly miserable. Any shops that we
could see were closed and the place seemed devoid of any interesting
features whatsoever. All passengers were herded into a large bleak
waiting room which, fortunately, was heated, but there was nothing
to do but wait until we could re-board and regain the comfort of our
compartment.

As we crossed the frozen expanse of Russia I reflected on books I
had read about the thousands of people who had been exiled to these
parts and of course to the one who exiled them – Stalin. Svetlana,
Stalin's daughter, who also recently died, was known to me and stayed
with us in London when she came to the UK with her daughter,
supposedly to settle. I first met her at a dinner party given by friends

in New York and when she eventually came to England, following the breakdown of her marriage to an American lawyer, she stayed in our guest flat for a while. Her daughter, an attractive and intelligent girl, needed to get into school and so I arranged to visit the Quaker school at Saffron Waldron with Svetlana to see if the girl might be admitted. She was but her mother was not happy, just as she was not happy about her life in general. I had deep sympathy for her, even though I had been told that eventually she would turn against anyone who offered her a helping hand. Eventually she blamed me for getting her daughter into an unsuitable school. One Orthodox Christmas she expressed a desire to go to the Russian Orthodox Church in London, then ministered to by the saintly Bishop Anthony Bloom. I said that I would accompany her but she felt she could not attend. 'If I go,' she said, 'everyone will recognize me and hate me because of my father.'

Many of her friends in the UK tried to dissuade her from leaving her home in Cambridge to return to Georgia in the then Soviet Union, but she was adamant. One day I called at the house to find it locked and bolted. She had gone. It was only a matter of months before she returned, having found it impossible to settle back in her home territory.

Life was hard for her. Understandably she was in a deep conflictual relationship with her father and there was little that one could do to help with that, apart from attempting to offer some friendship.

My own father, a strong disciplinarian, was someone whom I really did not get to know until he became seriously ill with cancer. I recollect clearly the day he told me that he had seen a specialist but the consultant had not given him any details as to the true nature of the illness. I asked him if he would like me to speak with the doctor on his behalf and he said that he would. When I eventually got through to the oncologist I was told that my father had cancer of the lung and only had a matter of months to live. 'Have you told him?' I asked. 'No' was the reply. 'Do you intend to tell him?' I said. 'No,' he replied again. I then asked if I should tell him and he said that he left the decision to me.

I decided that it was right to share with him what I had been told by the consultant and the fact that I did enabled us to have a relationship that we had not previously experienced. At first he was incredulous, but gradually came to the realization that he was in the last days of his life and accordingly put his affairs in order.

At the time I was living many miles away from Cheshire, where he lived with my mother, but nevertheless tried to visit him weekly. On the one weekend I could not get away he died. The following inadequate lines express something of my own grief at his passing.

### MY FATHER

It was the depth of night.
The time when one hovers
Between mortal life
And the unknown.
I stood by the bedside,
Fatigued
From driving.
The room was full
With the silence of death.

Cautiously
I drew back the sheet
Covering my father's face.
Brow furrowed.

Cheeks hollow.
Eyes closed.

Tears burned my eyes
As I wept
And remembered
Times past.
The time when he wept
As I told him
His death was near.
Now
Time has no meaning for him.
Released
From a body
Racked by pain
He has gone.
My father.
Daddy.
Gone . . .

There is one final story for this book concerning the Orthodox Cathedral in London. On my release I went to the morning service as I had done occasionally when in London before my captivity. At the end of the service, as is the custom, the congregation gathered around the Bishop as he delivered a short homily. He had obviously recognized me and said quite spontaneously, 'Welcome home. We have been praying for you and now we shall sing.' Immediately the whole congregation intoned the most beautiful Russian melody and reduced me to tears. Afterward I was told that on a visit I had made to the church just before being captured, Irina Ratushinskaya, the poet, was in the congregation following her release from imprisonment by the Soviets.

It is the Queen's Diamond Jubilee weekend and I am
in our old house in Suffolk. As the rain poured out of
the sky, I watched something of the Jubilee procession
along the Thames on the television and thought back
across the years to when I watched the Coronation
procession on my parents' little black and white set. It
was raining then, as it is raining now. Little did I think
then that I would eventually meet most members of the
Royal Family and even have a very minor role behind
the scenes in some of the great occasions of state.

Before my wife arrived from London with our dogs,
I sat at the kitchen table and wrote the following words.
I decided to include them, for what they are worth.
They are just a memory. A scrap of a memory.

### JUBILEE

It is hard to write
About majesty.
Clichés fly around,
Waiting to be seized
And fastened to the page.

I see them now.
'Jubilee',
'Union flag',
Personified
On painted face
And cheap tin tray.

London wakes.
A leaden sky
Recalls

Days imprisoned in memory.
'Watch carefully,'
Urged my father,
'You may never see the like again.'

The small screen flickered,
Portraying
An endless procession
Riding,
Marching,
Through rain-soaked streets
Bedecked
With sodden emblems.

Today,
Jubilee.
Six parts of a century
Have ebbed away.
My father?
Long dead.
The flickering screen?
No more.

Again I watch
The same emblems,
The same military colour,
The same relentless sky.
The same monarch,
Transformed by years,
Revered as Queen.

Slowly
The grey blanket
Of water

Is touched
With colour.
Red,
White,
Blue,
Gold,
Purple
Breathe life
To the leaden stream.
Music drifts from bank
To bank,
As monarch
And retinue
Glide along
Into the unknown.

Today
The nation gathered
To capture the past,
To find meaning
For today
And seize hope for tomorrow.

Jubilee

Jubilee in the rain

When it was first put to me by a friend that I ought
to consider publishing some of my attempts at poetry
I was hesitant, and now that I have committed some
of them to the printed page I still have my doubts.
It is only because of the repeated insistence of those
who have read them that I have got so far as to put
together this slim volume. If you have read this far
you will have taken a ramble through some of the
various pathways that have constituted my life. I could
fill many more pages with accounts of travels and
encounters made during the past 60 or so years. That,
I consider, would be self-indulgent on the one hand,
but on the other it might be justified as it would leave
a record for my children and grandchildren, for whom
I have the greatest affection.

The discerning reader will no doubt have realized
that I am a complicated mixture of introversion and
extraversion with feelings that run deep. My life has
been, and continues to be, something of a ramble and
at times I am amazed that I have managed to survive
as long as I have! I have not given myself away easily
and still remain a very private individual. I would
never have fitted into a conventional occupation and
indeed there are many, perhaps myself included, who
wonder what on earth it is that I do. Well, as I stumble
along life's pathway, I am always trying to understand
and interpret the mystery.

Unquestionably my childhood formation brought me
to religion, which provided an interpretative framework
for existence. I don't recollect a time when I took my

understanding of faith literally, and it is certainly true that as the years have passed I cannot possibly give a literal interpretation to traditional Christianity. And yet the pageant of the Orthodox liturgy or the beauty of an Anglican Choral Evensong still has great significance for me. However, it is in the stillness of corporate silence, as experienced in a Quaker meeting, that I discover a new depth of meaning. Here, apart from the simple conventions that guide the meeting, one has to face the deep pools of silence that both lie within and also exist across the great universe of which we are all a constituent part. It is in this experience that one realizes that we are the creators. We create or destroy. We fill the silence with meaning, or alternatively are lost in the depths of emptiness. In this vast mysterious universe there are many ways of understanding and interpreting truth and my effort to explore that particular mystery will continue until I depart this mortal life. As I stumble onwards a single line from the verse of a hymn comes to mind: 'Interpreted by love'. If I were to make one dogmatic statement it would be that love, in all its various forms, is a fundamental operative principle. It cannot be denied that the exposition of love contained in Chapter 13 of the letter to the Corinthians is as good a summary of love as one may hope for.

This last poem, an epitaph I suppose, speaks of a happy circumstance, alas all too rare, where two people have touched something of the mystery and reality of love.

## DO NOT FORGET ME

Do not forget me
When I am old.
Do not forget
That we loved with
A passion
That took us
Away from this
World,
Lost in each other,
Lost in a realm
Where in giving
We received
More than we
Could ever hope for.

Do not forget me
When I have departed
This life.
Hold me in your
Heart,
For we shall be
Together
And death
Will not part.

# Will you help a prisoner to avoid reoffending?

## Over forty per cent of prisoners have a reading level below that of the average 11-year-old. (National Literacy Trust, 2008)

This makes it very difficult for prisoners to find work when they get out of prison. But if they can go straight into a job on release, they are **nine times** less likely to end up back inside.

When we heard this, we wanted to give prisoners a chance to improve their skills, so we produced a series of fiction books just for them. Prisoners can identify with the believable heroes of these gritty stories. At the same time, questions for discussion at the end of each chapter explore choice, personal responsibility and the value of positive relationships (another key factor in preventing reoffending).

These books are making a real difference to the prisoners themselves, and chaplains, librarians and others who work in prisons love them. In the prisoners' own words:

> **Reading your book made me think how selfish I was towards other people and that I only thought of myself.**
> *Prisoner, HMP Bure*

> **This is the most realistic book I've ever read when it comes to leaving jail. The writer nails it – all the boys loved it!**
> *Prisoner, HMP Moorland*

You can help to support prisoners in improving their reading and their chances by donating now at **http://spckpublishing. co.uk/support-spck/** or by sending a cheque payable to SPCK to: **SPCK, 36 Causton Street, London SW1P 4ST.**

> **I learned to read in prison, and it turned my life around. I know more than anyone just how important this programme could be to someone inside.**
> *Lord Bird MBE, founder of* The Big Issue

CPSIA information can be obtained
at www.ICGtesting.com
Printed in the USA
BVHW041348280921
617682BV00019B/663